THE MOUNTAINS OF NERJA

About the Author

Jim Ryan is a chartered civil engineer with a passion for the outdoors. He has published several successful guidebooks and one work of fiction.

Jim's approach to guidebook writing is not simply to take the reader to the destination but to provide them with a total experience. Geology, the natural environment and the folklore and history of the locality are very important to him. Jim splits his time between Cork in Ireland and Nerja in Spain. He has been climbing the mountains of Nerja for over 15 years. This guidebook is his way of repaying Nerja and Andalucía for many years of pleasure. His share of the proceeds from this book go to Cudeca, a cancer hospice charity in the province of Malaga.

Other Cicerone guides by the author
Aconcagua and the Southern Andes

THE MOUNTAINS OF NERJA
SIERRAS DE TEJEDA, ALMIJARA Y ALHAMA
by Jim Ryan

JUNIPER HOUSE, MURLEY MOSS,
OXENHOLME ROAD, KENDAL, CUMBRIA LA9 7RL
www.cicerone.co.uk

© Jim Ryan 2014
First edition 2014
ISBN: 978 1 85284 754 8
Reprinted 2017 (with updates)

Printed in China on behalf of Latitude Press Ltd

A catalogue record for this book is available from the British Library.
Cartographic base 1:25,000 © National Geographic Institute of Spain
All photographs are by the author unless otherwise stated.

Acknowledgements

This guidebook is dedicated to the people of Nerja and surrounding towns and villages from whom I have derived tremendous camaraderie, friendship and cooperation. My late wife, Sue, was my inspiration and she proofread the initial issue. My new partner, Birgit, was my companion on many of the walks and I thank her for her assistance. Richard Mills, bird photographer extraordinaire, supplied the image of the Griffon vulture in Walk 14 and the peregrine falcon in Walk 19.

Updates to this Guide

While every effort is made by our authors to ensure the accuracy of guidebooks as they go to print, changes can occur during the lifetime of an edition. Any updates that we know of for this guide will be on the Cicerone website (www.cicerone.co.uk/754/updates), so please check before planning your trip. We also advise that you check information about such things as transport, accommodation and shops locally. Even rights of way can be altered over time. We are always grateful for information about any discrepancies between a guidebook and the facts on the ground, sent by email to updates@cicerone.co.uk or by post to Cicerone, 2 Police Square, Milnthorpe LA7 7PY, United Kingdom.

Front cover: Climbers on Almendrón with the iconic almond-shaped tower in the background

CONTENTS

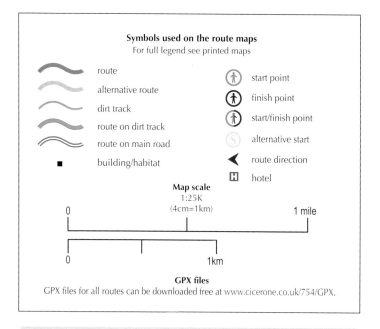

Symbols used on the route maps

For full legend see printed maps

route		start point
alternative route		finish point
dirt track		start/finish point
route on dirt track		alternative start
route on main road		route direction
building/habitat		hotel

Map scale
1:25K
(4cm=1km)

0   1 mile

0   1km

GPX files
GPX files for all routes can be downloaded free at www.cicerone.co.uk/754/GPX.

Mountain Warning

Mountain walking can be a dangerous activity carrying a risk of personal injury or death. It should be undertaken only by those with a full understanding of the risks and with the training and experience to evaluate them. While every care and effort has been taken in the preparation of this guide, the user should be aware that conditions can be highly variable and can change quickly, materially affecting the seriousness of a mountain walk. Therefore, except for any liability that cannot be excluded by law, neither Cicerone nor the author accept liability for damage of any nature (including damage to property, personal injury or death) arising directly or indirectly from the information in this book.

To call out the Mountain Rescue, ring the international emergency number 112: this will connect you via any available network. The telephone number for the police throughout Spain is 091.

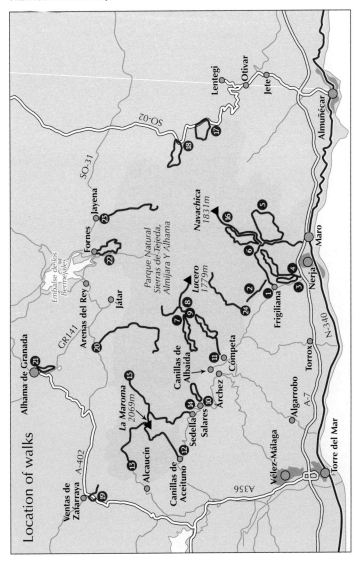

Location of walks

INTRODUCTION

The little seaside town of Nerja nestles under a range of mighty mountains that stretch to the north, away from the coast. Hillwalkers internationally have recently begun to realise what treasures lie in this region. Although these mountains are well-known locally in Spain, the neighbouring mountains of the Alpujarras and the Sierra Nevada to the east have up until now been the better recognised attractions for the outdoor fraternity of northern Europe.

However, by 2011, the ever-increasing numbers of visitors coming to the Sierras Tejeda, Almijara and Alhama led the government of Andalucía to build a state-of-the-art interpretive centre at Sedella in the south and expand the interpretive centre near Fornes in the north, and their 2011 guide to the area (in Spanish) is now widely distributed. Today, walkers with their boots, rucksacks and walking sticks are a common sight in the town of Nerja and the neighbouring villages of Cómpeta, Frigiliana and Canillas de Albaida.

Here there are over fifty mountains over 3000ft (914m) (equivalent to the Scottish Munros), in an area about the size of the Isle of Skye. The highest of these mountains is over 2000m, and a significant number are taller than Ben Nevis. Many of the mountains have maintained and waymarked paths.

To climb the mountains of Scotland and Ireland hillwalkers need to consider that summits will be in cloud 70 to 80 per cent of the time; by contrast, in Andalucía the figure is more like ten per cent. Spain is also one of the most affordable countries in Europe to visit and there is a universal welcome for the visitor.

The aim of this guide is to provide accurate information and route directions for independent walkers, with lots of background information to make their explorations of this stunning area even more rewarding.

GEOGRAPHICAL CONTEXT

Nerja is a small coastal town 60km east of Malaga, presided over to the north by the Almijaras. The Almijaras are orientated on an east-west axis and they join the Sierra Tejeda to the west and the smaller Sierra Alhama further to the northwest. There are three other minor sierras on the periphery of the region. The foothills of the Sierra Nevada, the Alpujarras, are some 80km to the northeast.

The wider region in which the routes described in this book sit is referred to in Spanish as the Axarquía, which comes from Moorish and means the 'lands to the east'. The principle towns of the Axarquía are Vélez-Málaga and Nerja but Nerja

The gorge of Alhama (Walk 21)

On the path to Lucero (Walk 8)

is the one chosen as the focus of this guide because it is closest to the centre of the mountains and many of the walks included begin there. The official name for the area, promoted by the Andalucían Tourist Board, is Sierras Tejeda, Almijara Y Alhama, which is also the name of the national park. However, most people, Spanish included, may find this title rather challenging.

THE TOWN OF NERJA

Nerja has a population of 22,000, which grows in the summer to several times this number with the influx of tourists. Many of the properties in the town are unoccupied outside the tourist season. The town is well-known throughout Spain because *Verano Azul*, a popular soap opera on Spanish television some years ago, was based here. Today 20 per cent of the permanent residents of Nerja are foreigners who have relocated mainly from northern Europe, typically England, Sweden, Germany, the Netherlands, Ireland and Belgium.

The town is a maze of narrow streets that all seem to lead towards the Balcón de Europa, a public square on a promontory above the Mediterranean.

There is no beach of any size in the centre of town, but on the outskirts of the town, to the east and west, there are fine beaches. Nerja boasts many

11

quality medium-priced hotels, hostels and apartments to rent, and there are numerous excellent restaurants, bars and nightclubs. Most of the hotels cater for group bookings and there are discounts in the off-peak seasons.

One of the principle tourist attractions is the Cave of Nerja. Situated immediately northeast of the town, this limestone cave has five kilometres of chambers, many of magnificent proportions, which were inhabited as far back as 25,000 years ago.

The white mountain villages

Frigiliana, Cómpeta, Canillas de Albaida, Canillas de Aceituno and Salares are just some of the quaint, white-painted villages a short distance from Nerja. Several others are visited on the walks. These villages have a history that spans the occupations by the Romans and the Moors and they still pursue old customs and a pace of life that reflects the traditions of rural Spain.

GEOLOGY AND TOPOGRAPHY

The mountains of Nerja are largely limestone, but they span 500 million years of geological time. The youngest rocks are the conglomerates that can be seen below the Balcón de Europa, which are only 10,000 years old. The walk to Haza de la Encina, south of Jayena (Walk 23), crosses Pliocene conglomerates that are five million years old. The cliffs of Alhama de Granada (Walk 21) are from the Miocene and so are about 15 million years old. Then we jump back in time to the Jurassic

Typical street in Frigiliana

Lucerillo 1690m   Lucero 1774m   La Cruz del Pinto 365m   Cisne 1483m

The Almijaras mountains above the town of Nerja (L: Western; R: Eastern)

rocks, 180 million years old, for the climb at Ventas de Zafarraya (Walk 19). But the oldest rocks are those that form the main body of the mountains of Nerja and these are 280 to 500 million years in age, spanning geological periods from the Permian back through the Carboniferous and into the Cambrian.

The older rocks were lifted and the mountains formed 30 million years ago during the tectonic collision of a Mediterranean breakaway plate with the land masses of Africa and Europe. This collision caused the formation of the Betic Cordillera of which Sierra Nevada, the Alpujarras and the mountains of Nerja are a part.

Earthquakes

The mountains of Nerja are in the most active seismic area on the Iberian Peninsula and experience major earthquakes roughly every hundred years. The most notable in relatively recent times was on Christmas Day in 1884 when a tremor measured

Nerja's Balcón de Europa

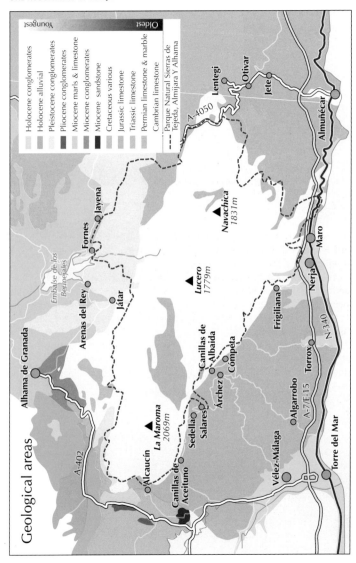

Geological areas

Youngest — Oldest

Holocene conglomerates
Holocene alluvial
Pleistocene conglomerates
Pliocene conglomerates
Miocene marls & limestone
Miocene conglomerates
Miocene sandstone
Cretaceous various
Jurassic limestone
Triassic limestone
Permian limestone & marble
Cambrian limestone
--- Parque Natural Sierras de Tejeda, Almijara Y Alhama

Lentegi
Otivar
Jete
Almuñécar
A-4050
Jayena
Fornes
Navachica 1831m
Maro
Nerja
Embalse de los Bermejales
Arenas del Rey
Játar
Lucero 1779m
Frigiliana
N-340
Canillas de Albaida
Compéta
Torrox
Alhama de Granada
Árchez
Algarrobo
A-7/E-15
A-402
Sedella
Salares
Alcaucín
La Maroma 2069m
Vélez-Málaga
Torre del Mar
Canillas de Aceituno

14

Karst limestone

at 6.5 on the Richter Scale hit, with its epicentre northeast of Canillas de Aceituno. It affected every village and town in the Axarquía, killing 745 people. Further tremors occurred in January and minor aftershocks were felt throughout the following year. The devastation was compounded by heavy snows in the mountains. The King of Spain visited the region, was taken ill and died soon afterwards. The most recent tremors were recorded in 1956 and 2003.

The limestone varies from white soft chalk to hard, blue calcitic rocks. In the area of Fuente del Esparto there are lenses of black limestone shales, while near Lucero the heat from the mountain building has turned the limestone into marble. There are no volcanic rocks in this region.

There are areas where the limestone is friable, reminiscent of the

Dolomites, and other areas where they are Karstic, with holes cut into the rock by acidic solution. The entire area is dotted with caves of all shapes and sizes.

The mountains consist of a main chain stretching from La Maroma (2069m) in the west through Cerro Santiago (1646m), Malascamas (1792m), Cerro la Chapa (1820m), Lucero (1775m), La Cadena (1645m) to Navachica (1832m) and Lopera (1485m) in the east. South of the main chain is a series of foothills of which El Fuerte (1007m), Tres Cruces (1204m) and Cerro Atalaya (1255m) are examples. At Navachica the mountain range opens into a three-pronged fork with Cerro Cisne (1483m) on the eastern limb, Tajo Almendrón (1515m) in the middle and El Cielo (1508m) on the western limb.

A LITTLE HISTORY

Spanish history is extremely complex and very difficult to summarise so only a brief overview can be given here.

The earliest evidence of human beings in Europe was found in Spain. In a cave near Zaffaraya in 1933, bones were discovered that are believed to have belonged to Neanderthal Man, dating to 30,000 years ago. There is also evidence of prehistoric life in the Cave of Nerja. Near Fornes in the extreme north of the region there is a passage grave that has been dated to the Neolithic period. The Iberian Peninsula is known to have been visited by the

Roman aqueduct at Torrecuevas (Valley of Rio Verde)

Phoenicians and the Greeks before the arrival of the Romans, some 200 years BC. Hispania, as it was then known, was ruled from Rome for 600 years.

From around 400AD to 700AD the peninsula was conquered by the Visigoths, who were subsequently replaced by the Moors. These Muslims ruled Spain until the early 13th century, when the Catholic Conquest began. In the Axarquía there was considerable Moorish influence. It can be seen today in the Alhambra in Granada. Mudegar architecture is widespread and all towns and villages with names beginning with 'al' betray their Moorish origins. The climate in Andalucía was ideal for the silk industry set up by the Moors. Even to this day we can see the Arabic features in the people of Andalucía more than in the rest of Spain.

During the Muslim period there were three main religious groups – the Muslims, the Christians and the Jews. Strangely enough the Jews allied themselves to the Muslims and lived in close proximity to them as their protectors from the Christians. After the Catholic conquest all people were required to convert to Christianity or face death or expulsion. The majority of the Muslims did so convert and were then known as Moriscos, but the Jews substantially packed their bags and left the country.

From late in the 19th century to the beginning of the First World War Spain was torn between disputes

Cabras montés

over the monarchy, a republic and dictatorship. During the Spanish Civil War and for many years after it in Andalucía, and particularly in the Axarquía district, there were many enclaves of republicans who resisted the dictator General Franco, and there were many bloody encounters. The mountains visited on these walks were ideal refuges for the Maqui, the republican sympathisers, to hide in.

A good introduction to the history and culture of the region is *La Axarquía – Land to the East of Málaga* by Hilary Gavilan (see Appendix D).

WILDLIFE

The wildlife and plants of the Spanish hillsides are truly remarkable and very different from those of northern Europe. There are very few dangerous creatures about, and where there are they will be as nervous of you as you are of them.

The *cabras montés* are only found in the Iberian Peninsula and the vast concentration of them is in the Axarquía. You will glimpse them all the time but these wild goats with deerskin hides are very shy and will

Processionary caterpillars

17

move away from intruders. They are extremely agile and will often be seen travelling up and down slopes at great speed. In the area around La Resinera, you may also encounter red deer.

Seeing wild cats, foxes and hares will be a rarity. Similarly, snakes are shy and infrequently encountered. There are many birds of prey to be spotted hovering in the skies, including kestrels, falcons, vultures and even eagles.

The most dangerous insects in Spain are processionary caterpillars. They make their woven white nests in the branches of pine trees and emerge in lines that may be several metres in length. However docile they may seem, they can eject a nasty poison from their hairy backs.

Flor de Jara

PLANTS AND FLOWERS

The mountain flowers come to life in the springtime, when many familiar species and others that are particular to the Mediterranean will be better seen. On the slopes of El Fuerte the exotic Flor de Jara thrives. This bush is related to Cistus – Rock Rose, and it likes lime-rich soil. Where the Spanish name for a plant or flower mentioned in the route descriptions is available it is given, and some of these are very interesting. For example, the poppy in Spain is an *amapola* (wet land); broom is *lluvia de oro* (rain of gold).

The most common tree to be seen on these walks is the pine tree. However, in the past yew trees

predominated here. Sierra Tejeda takes its name from the Spanish word for yew, *tejo*. The yews were cut down because they were considered to be poisonous to livestock and pines were planted in their place to expand the resin industry. The demise of the yews is highlighted in the interpretive centres and a programme has commenced to replace some of them. The pines are well adapted to withstand drought. The red berried prickly juniper features on the Almendrón walk (Walk 6). Holm Oaks – the evergreen Holly Oak – have adapted here to survive the dry summers.

If you want to read more about Spanish wildflowers, two field guides are recommended in Appendix D.

GETTING TO NERJA

Nerja is 40 minutes by car from the city of Malaga. The airport at Malaga is one of the busiest in Spain with flights into it from almost every country in Europe. Easyjet (www.easyjet.com), Ryanair (www.ryanair.com), Monarch (www.monarch.co.uk) and British Airways (www.britishairways.co.uk)

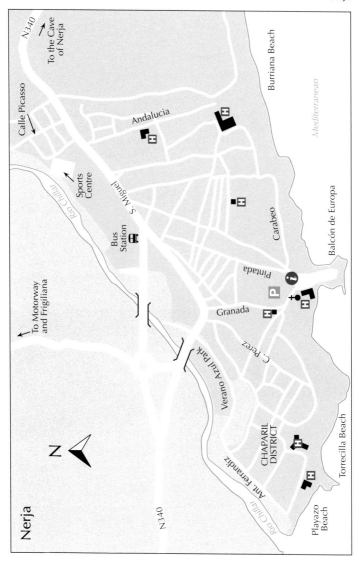

Nerja

N

N340

To Motorway and Frigiliana

Río Chillar

Sports Centre

Río Chillar

N340

Calle Picasso

To the Cave of Nerja

Andalucia

S. Miguel

Bus Station

Burriana Beach

Mediterranean

Balcón de Europa

Carabeo

Pintada

Granada

C. Perez

Verano Azul Park

Avml. Ferrandiz

CHAPARIL DISTRICT

Torrecilla Beach

Playazo Beach

all operate regular flights to Malaga from various cities in the UK. From outside the airport terminal there is a regular shuttle bus into the main bus station in Malaga, from where there are regular buses to Nerja. The fares on these buses are remarkably cheap.

Car rental companies (such as Malagacar, www.malagacar.com) vie for custom at the airport, but it will be more economical to compare prices online and make a booking before arrival. Some companies rent their cars with a full tank of fuel and ask for it to be returned empty; an obvious advantage for them since returning it empty is rather impractical. There are a number of car rental companies in Nerja (such as Autos Tívoli, www. autostivoli.com), but their rates are generally not as competitive as those

at the airport. Many of the approaches to the walks in this book involve driving on dirt roads so you may prefer to rent a high wheelbase car or even a small offroader.

A taxi from the airport and back is likely to be costlier than hiring a car, but there are companies (all in Nerja) that ferry people on a taxi-sharing basis.

The airport at Almeria to the east is more than an hour from Nerja and is not served as well with buses and car rentals.

Malaga can also be accessed by train or bus from the cities of Madrid, Seville and Cadiz. Spanish train timetables can be checked and tickets bought online at www.renfe.com and bus times and tickets are available at www.alsa.es.

The kiosk in Frigiliana

ACCOMMODATION

All the routes in this guide could be done in a single day trip from Nerja, so Nerja is a good place to base yourself for your trip. There are hotels in Nerja that specialise in group bookings for walkers. Since walkers generally come in the spring or autumn, out-of-season rates apply. These hotels operate on a bed, breakfast, packed lunch and evening meal basis, or on variations of these.

The hotels specialising in catering for walking groups tend to be medium to small hotels, but there are a few luxury establishments in the town as well. Equally there are hostels that are economic and operate on a bed and breakfast arrangement. A useful source of information about accommodation in Nerja is www.nerjatoday. com.

For those who want to fend for themselves, Nerja has many empty apartments available to rent in the off season. Almost all of the real estate agencies in the town provide this service. The option of renting and eating out is very practical, for there are numerous cafés and restaurants that open early and serve anything from coffee and rolls to a full English breakfast. For evening meals there is a wide choice – English roasts, Italian pastas, Indian curries, Mexican spices and many fine establishments serving the best of Spanish cuisine.

The choice of accommodation location lies between proximity to the town centre, the beaches and the mountains. Nerja town centre is a maze of narrow one-way streets, decidedly not car-friendly. So, cars may have to be parked remotely from accommodation.

The bus from Malaga arrives at the top, or eastern end, of the town. It is a 10-minute, downhill walk to most places within the town, but there is a taxi rank at the bus station.

WHEN TO GO

Officially it has never rained in living memory in Nerja during June, July and August. However, as well as being dry during these months, the weather is hot and the town is packed with tourists. In this high season everything is that little bit more expensive. While the coast is basking in heat the mountains tend to be shrouded in cloud. The Nerjans say that the town has its own microclimate such that it never gets unbearably hot and does not suffer from the high humidity of other coastal towns.

For the hillwalker the best time to go is in late April and early May. There may be a little snow on Maroma, but otherwise the temperature is ideal for walking: not too hot and with little threat of rain. The flowers will be in full bloom and the landscape will be green. In early April the flowers will be out, but the rainy season has not yet concluded. The two biggest festivals in the town take place over Easter and on 15 May. Religious processions are big throughout Andalucía, when a

In the spring, the paths on the north side of La Maroma can be covered in snow

significant proportion of the townsfolk take part. Spanish tourists pour into the town to witness the dedication that the community has to its processions. The spectacle is a moving one.

In late summer and early autumn the weather will again be very suitable for walking, but after the hot summer the land will be brown and scorched. From November through to April walking in Andalucía is still very acceptable, although you are now more prone to rain and possibly snow on Maroma. There will be more water in the rivers, many of which must be crossed on the walks, so that getting feet wet may become inevitable. Snow on the Almijaras is rare,

with Navachica the most vulnerable. There is never any snow on Lucero because the high winds remove it, but there can be snow on the northern approach to its summit.

The dirt track road into Pinarillo and Fuente del Esparto is (sometimes) closed from 1 June to 1 October, because of the threat of forest fires. This adds considerably to the length of Walks 5, 6 and 16 and this is indicated in the route descriptions.

WALKING IN ANDALUCÍA

The Andalucían Parque Nacional has set up and now maintains designated walking trails, and many of the walks in this book follow such trails. The paths are often old mining routes or former mule tracks through the mountains. All of these maintained paths are waymarked. They have a sign at the start of the walk (in Spanish) with notes on what you are about to encounter, a little history, the distance and time it will take and the relative difficulty. It is important to note that the time given on these signs is always for a one-way trip and does not include your return to the start.

The waymarks indicate the direction; where other paths link there are waymarks with crosses to show that they are not to be followed. All waymarked paths have relatively moderate gradients. For the experienced walker this can be a little frustrating because the route is extended to maintain the gentle gradient and becomes laboriously long. In this book shortcuts have been adopted for the most excessive cases.

Many of the walks are not on waymarked trails, which tend to be more challenging. Over time paths can be subject to change: from earthworks, landslides, river flooding and vegetation encroachment and so on, so that you need to keep your wits about you.

The most important thing is to find the start of the path and be sure that it is the correct path. Once you are on a path all you need to do is follow it. Wandering off the path is generally not an option because of the surrounding vegetation.

Almost all the land in this area is in public ownership and is part of

The path into the Rio Verde valley (Walk 17)

the national park. The exceptions are areas immediately north of Frigiliana, part of the Rio Verde Valley, the eastern walk of Ventas de Zafarraya, and land north of Maroma. There are signs indicating when land is private and none of the routes in this book require you to trespass on private land where it is so indicated (although Walk 20 does follow a public right of way that passes through private land).

SPANISH DIALECT IN ANDALUCÍA

The Andalucíans have many peculiarities in their speech that differ from the Castellaño that is spoken in Madrid. The language sounds much smoother here, not as harsh as that of their northern neighbours and more akin to the Spanish of South America.

For example, the word 'Andalucía' is pronounced as it would be in English, whereas in Madrid it would be 'Andaluthia'. The English pronunciation of the name 'Nerja' is 'Nerka', but to be more correct it is 'Nerha', with the 'h' pronounced gutterally.

The river that flows through the town is the Rio Chillar, which is pronounced Chiyar, because two 'l's are pronounced as a 'y' in Spanish.

In Andalucía there is a tendency to drop all 's's in the middle and endings of words. So to buy two beers (*dos cervecas*) the request would be 'dos thervethas' in Madrid. In Nerja, 'doe cervaytha' will be heard, or for

three it will be 'tray'. To ask how a person is one would say 'como estas' in Madrid, but in Nerja it would be 'como ayta', both of the 's's having been dropped.

The Spanish pronounce all of their vowels individually (not as dipthongs, as native English-speakers do). So the unit of currency is an 'ayuro' and the mountain of El Fuerte is pronounced 'El Fuuertay'.

RECURRING PLACE NAMES

There is a degree of repetition in the names of geographical features. There is a Puerto Blanquillo and a Puerta Blanquilla; there are at least two Salto de Caballos, two El Fuerte mountains and a couple of Cerro Verdes; one set of peaks is known as Los Dos Hermanos (the two brothers), a col on Cisne is known as Collado de los Dos Hermanos, while another peak is called Las Dos Hermanas (the two sisters). To the north of the region there is the town of Arenas del Rey, while nearer the coast there is the village of Arenas. But as long as you know where you are, there should be no cause for confusion!

MAPS AND GPS COORDINATES

Topografica publish the official National Geographic Institute of Spain (IGN) 1:50,000 and 1:25,000 maps of the area laid out to the 1950 European UTM grid. These maps are relatively inexpensive to buy but are not widely

Red deer

available. The quality of paper is poor and all paths are not shown on them. For some of the walks more than one map will be required. They can be purchased direct at a shop in Malaga, or they can be purchased online (see Appendix E, 'Maps of the region'). See Appendix C for a glossary of useful words for map reading.

The *Axarquía Tour and Trail* 1:40,000 published by Discovery Walking Guides is quite a clear map, but the October 2010 version has many little mistakes (for instance, Frigiliana and Canillas de Aceituno are misspelled, and there are a number of features that are out of place). Unfortunately the 2010 version is to an imperial grid.

A GPS is not essential for most of the walks. There is often not a great deal of point in giving waypoint coordinates. The key thing is to find the start of the walk and stick to the path. However, for walkers who prefer to carry a GPS device of some sort, some waypoints have been identified in the route descriptions at particularly critical navigational points. The GPS coordinates set out in the guide relate to the European Grid and are in metric. The coordinates given, for example,

25

215:420760:4087650, are made up of **height** in metres: **easting** in metres and **northing** in metres.

Some summary information is provided at the start of each route description to help you select the right walk for you and your party. This includes the total distance, the total height gain, a rough estimate of the time a walk might take (allowing for reasonable rests and refreshment breaks), a difficulty rating and directions for getting to the start of the walk from the nearest town or village. Other options for your day in that particular area are also suggested in some cases. There is also a summary table in Appendix A to help you compare the different routes.

Route maps

The routes are marked onto 1:25,000 IGN base maps, except for detailed navigation through villages where street maps, with scales indicated, are provided. The main route line is marked in orange and variants are marked in blue. There are some inaccuracies in the base maps and so in some cases key features have been marked over the top in heavier black type with an arrow to pinpoint the correct location.

The approach to Collado de Dos Hermanos on Cisne (Walk 24). The mark on the rock shows that there is only 100m of climbing left, but it is the most difficult 100 metres

GPX files for all the routes described here are available for anyone who has bought this guide to download free from the Cicerone website. Just go to www.cicerone.co.uk/member. All the official Spanish mapping is also now available to buy, by map tile, province or region, for use within the ViewRanger navigation app on tablets, phones and other devices.

Difficulty

The difficulty rating given for each route is on a scale of one to ten with the higher numbers reserved for long and strenuous walks. A route with a difficulty rating of 1 would be suitable for children and grandparents and where ordinary sports shoes would be appropriate, while one rated 10 should be reserved only for those who are very fit, in good walking boots and with all the essential gear for eventualities in the mountains, and, of course, the stamina for long and strenuous walking. The climb of Cisne poses particular risks that are set out in the notes for that walk.

All of the walks are suitable for regular hillwalkers.

What to take

During hot months in the mountains it is essential to bring an adequate quantity of water or other fluid. ('Adequate' will vary from person to person but 1–2 litres per person is a good rule of thumb when exerting yourself in a hot climate.) Water

False smooth snake

sources on the walks are generally poor to non-existent.

Wearing shorts will be appropriate on many of the easier walks, but for the more difficult walks through thick and spiky vegetation long trousers or leggings are required. This particularly applies to Walks 1, 5, 6 and 16, and the eastern section of Walk 19.

You could encounter snakes on any of the walks in this book but it is highly unlikely. They will be more scared of you than you are of them and will keep well away if they can. However, it may be wise to wear gaiters in areas of thick vegetation. On the walk on El Cielo, in particular, ankle protection is recommended, because you will not be able to see the ground clearly on the first half of the walk.

A view down over Fornes (Walk 22)

The routes in this book are not technical. The only walk for which roping up is recommended is the ascent of Cisne, at the point of the traverse on the eastern side of the summit.

Likewise, a GPS is not necessary for most of the walks in this book. However, you should take one if you are going to tackle the walks to Almendrón (Walk 6), Navachica (Walk 16), Malascamas (Walk 20) and Cisne (Walk 24).

NERJA AND AROUND

The approach to the gorges (Walk 4)

WALK 1
Frigiliana to the Cave of Nerja

Start	Plaza Ingenio, Frigiliana
Finish	The Cave of Nerja
Distance	15km (as far as the east side of Nerja); 18km including the extension to La Presa dam; 11km taking the shortcut to El Pinarillo
Difficulty	3
Time	5½ hrs; 6hrs including the dam; 4½ hrs taking the shortcut
Height gain	600m
Getting to the start	The most practical way of getting to the start of this walk is to take a bus from Nerja to Frigiliana. Regular buses leave the bus station at the top of the town and, 15 minutes later, arrive at the main square, Plaza Ingenio, in Frigiliana.

This walk would make a good first excursion for getting a feel for the features and landmarks of the Nerja area. It crosses two rivers and skirts under some of the region's high peaks.

One of the Junta de Andalucía's waymarked walks, this route is maintained and easy to follow. It is an undulating and rough walk and a little steep in places. The first river crossing is unlikely to cause any difficulty, but the second may be ankle deep if the weather has been wet.

The ancient village of **Frigiliana** has a chequered past and was the centre for many industries over its history. Artefacts unearthed here include 3000-year-old Neolithic remains as well as Roman coins. It was a Moorish enclave for centuries and the scene of a bloody battle in 1569.

High up on the mountain of El Fuerte above the village there are the remains of two lime kilns, an indication of the old industry of producing

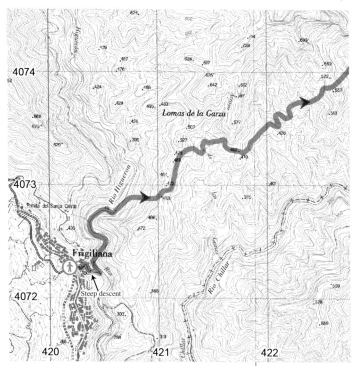

mortar and whitewash; the large old building on the main square, El Ingenio, The Engine, referred to the sugar factory that existed here from the early 17th century; the tourist office itself, Casa del Apero, the house of the farm implements, is 15th century.

The ceramic plaques of Frigiliana are most interesting and feature in Walk 2.

If you stand in the square facing the obvious tall building, you will see a decorative kiosk in the foreground. Behind the kiosk and off to the left is the stone path up to the centre of the old town. To the right, the stepped path in the opposite direction leads to the tourist office at Casa Del

Apero. In between these two opposing directions there is an alleyway with signs for the Rio Higueron, and this is the route.

The walk descends a steep concrete path down to the river bed. Just short of it there is a kerbed path on the left. Turn off onto this path. This is a disused concrete water channel, a regular feature of walks in this area, and following this instead of the river should keep your feet dry.

Going left against the flow of the Rio Higueron, the route passes by a reservoir and a grove of gum trees and presently arrives at the river crossing. (The river is usually a trickle here.)

Fringed pinks

There is a **noticeboard**, typical of all of the way-marked walks, here. It says that the distance is 6.3km; it will take three hours and the difficulty is medium (time and distance are one way and only as far as the Fuente del Esparto; it is quite a few kilometres further to Nerja). It says to take good boots and that the walk may be dangerous in winter when the mountains may suddenly be enveloped in cloud. It also describes the wonders of the gorges of the Rio Chillar and it suggests looking out for eagles and peregrine falcons in the skies. The advice is not to drink the water from either of the rivers.

From the signpost the trail rises steeply.

Looking up the river valley the high mountain in the distance that has its point flattened at the top is **Lucero** (1775m). With binoculars you should be able to see the ruins of a building at the top. Immediately to the left of Lucero is its little infant, Lucerillo (the one with the very pointed top). Across the valley from them is the flat plateau of La Cadena (1645m). A careful look shows that there is a sharp two-pronged feature in front of this plateau and this is Cerro Cisne. The mountain that the walk skirts immediately to the left is Cerro Capriote (1145m).

Walkers on the trail rising up from the river

The path gradually reaches a col from where the trail can be seen off to the right in the distance. The route is now descending down to the Rio Chillar, with a few ups and downs along the way. It wanders into narrow ravines and out onto open hillside, leading through rosemary, gorse, broom and esparto, and passing twisted pine trees.

Long before reaching the river, the sound of the water can be heard as it cascades down over mighty limestone boulders strewn in its path. Once you reach the river the trail is not very clear; it turns left to follow the bank of the river until the waymark on the opposite bank can be seen and you need to cross. There should be a shallow ford

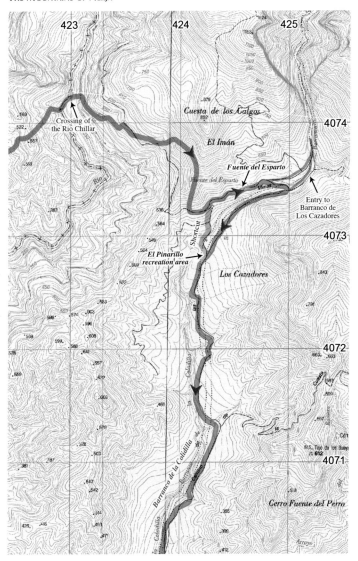

423   424   425

Crossing of
the Rió Chillar

Cuesta de los Galgos

El Imán

4074

Fuente del Esparto

Fuente del Esparto

Minas

Entry to
Barranco de
Los Cazadores

Shortcut

4073

El Pinarillo
recreation area

Los Cazadores

4072

Coladilla

4071

Barranco de la Coladilla

Cerro Fuente del Perro

Arroyo

here, but, if the river is in flood, be prepared for some delicate negotiation.

The trail rises steeply out of the valley of the Rio Chillar and passes over a river channel. This is the main water supply to the town of Nerja.

Extension to the dam at La Presa

The outflow of the river at La Presa, the dam, can be reached by taking the path to the left. This short diversion goes along the side of the channel, precipitous in places, but it provides a flavour of the enormous task that was undertaken in the 1950s to clamp this concrete channel to the sides of the mountains. The round trip to the dam will add half an hour to the journey.

Three kilometres further above the dam, in the area that is the source of the Rio Chillar, there is a small

Water supply channel

35

The Fuente del Esparto

building, **Cortijo Imán**, the farm of the holy Muslim man, renowned as an area where, in ancient times, tobacco was grown and illicitly marketed.

The path up from the water channel reaches a col where it joins a wide dirt-track road that goes to La Presa. Turning right, the route descends this road initially. The dirt track then takes a sharp left where there are other paths joining it, but the walk continues to follow the waymarks. Half a kilometre from this junction, and half a kilometre short of Fuente del Esparto, there is a path to the right.

Shortcut to El Pinarillo

This is where the walk-in for an ascent of Almendrón ends.

If your legs are tired you can take this path direct to El Pinarillo recreation area, shaving 4km off the distance. Follow the dirt track half a kilometre on to reach Fuente del Esparto. ◄

The old aqueduct

The Fuente del Esparto, or the Fountain of the High Grasses, is on the side of the trail. Unfortunately it is frequented by honey bees whose hives are above

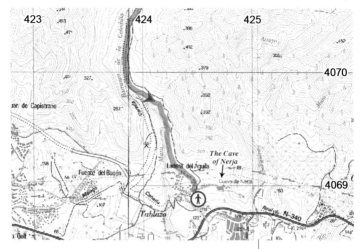

the fountain. So, to refill a water bottle requires a little courage.

Passing the fountain, the route arrives at the base of a ravine. This is the **Barranco de los Cazadores**, The Ravine of the Hunters, the beginning of the way up Almendrón. Follow the dirt track as it swings right after crossing the ravine. After about a kilometre, the road passes **El Pinarillo recreation area**, where you can get fresh water.

Several long kilometres further on, the track emerges onto the road up to the **Cave of Nerja**. From here, public buses into town are infrequent and catching a taxi is only a remote possibility. However, the walk into town is lined with many places of interest.

One feature en route is the area known as **La Fabrica**. The Factory, a very famous landmark in the town, was once a sugar factory with the lands surrounding it planted with sugar cane. In the early part of the 20th century a distillery was added and a very fine aqueduct was constructed to take water to it.

WALK 2
El Fuerte

Start/Finish	Plaza del Ingenio, Frigiliana; or reservoir car park, Pozo de Lizar
Distance	9km
Difficulty	4
Time	3½ hrs
Height gain	690m
Getting there	There are regular buses from Nerja that stop in the Plaza del Ingenio, the main square in the upper part of the village. If arriving by car drive through the village in the direction of Cómpeta and, after 1½ km, take the high road to the right, signposted to the Camino del Fuerte. This will lead to the reservoir where you can park.
Option	Walk back (6km; 1½ to 2hrs) from Frigiliana to Nerja via the Río Higueron

El Fuerte, 'the tough one', rises above and to the northwest of Frigiliana. This walk goes through the stepped narrow streets of this delightful white village and up the mountain for wonderful views over its tiled roofs to Nerja, down to Acebuchal and up to the high mountains. The climb follows a well-defined path with lots of opportunities for spotting mountain flowers.

THE MORISCOS' REBELLION

In 1569 a considerable number of moriscos lived in this area. These were Muslims who converted to Christianity, and this walk sets off through the *barrio* (district) *de moriscos*. The moriscos rebelled against the harsh conditions imposed on them and a Spanish army was dispatched to put down the rebellion. The ensuing conflict moved out of Frigiliana up the mountain. Many moriscos threw themselves to their deaths off El Fuerte rather than surrender.

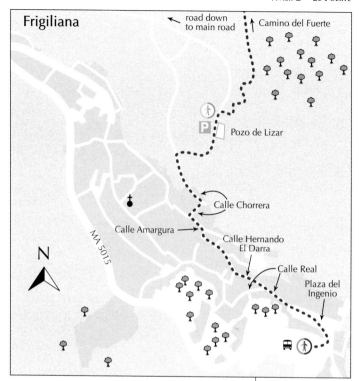

▶ The main street leading up the village from the Plaza del Ingenio is Calle Real. Head up this, always ascending and generally going to the right. (The route follows the ceramic plaques of Frigiliana, which can be examined on the return.)

Taking the first stepped option up right through Calle Hernando El Darra carry on into Calle Amargura. Avoiding the turn down Calle Santo Cristo go left until you reach and carry on into Calle Chorrera. This street will bend to the left and lead you from the cobblestone village street out onto a concrete road into the countryside.

There are no signposts to the Camino del Fuerte from the centre of the village but the locals all know the way, and, should you get lost, the enquiry will be an experience in itself.

39

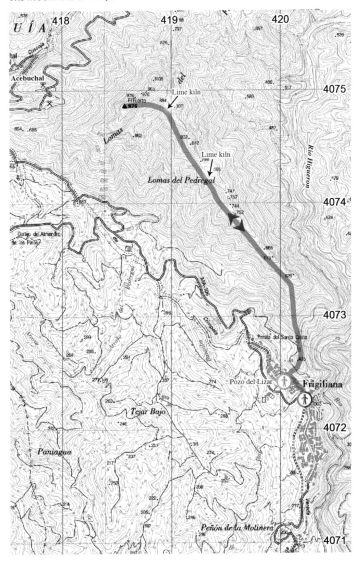

The route through Frigiliana

After a hundred metres there is a road junction where there is a high retaining wall of conglomerate stone on the right. The route turns sharp right up the steep concrete road until it arrives at a multiple junction. On the right is a pair of brick gateposts. On the left a rough path skirts around a grove of avocado trees. This is the path to the reservoir.

Take this path as it narrows and eventually emerges onto a road where you can hear the sounds of the water from the channel discharging into the reservoir. This area is known as **Pozo de Lizar** (*pozo* meaning well – water).

Turn left and follow the water channel to pass the first waymark on your right. This is the start of the Camino.

The walk follows a waymarked, stepped path that is steepest at the start and gradually develops into a gentler gradient.

The **solid limestone** is vertically bedded with a slight dip to the west and the distinct bedding planes in it can be seen. This limestone will contrast with the weathered limestone further up.

The path meanders through pine woodland and is bordered by rosemary and broom bushes.

The well-trodden path nears the summit

Kidney vetch

No matter what time of year there is always an abundance of **wildflowers** on El Fuerte. The low-lying kidney vetch (*vulneraria* in Spanish) may be seen at the sides of the path and blooms in the springtime, while the fringed pink (*clavellina* in Spanish) is an autumn flower. Worth looking out for is the cistus, or rock rose (*Flor de Jara* in Spanish), which is plentiful thanks to the mountain's lime-rich soil.

The well-trodden path passes the remains of a bee-hive stone structure on the right and at this point you are now halfway to the summit.

This stone structure is in fact the ruin of a **lime kiln**. Limestone was collected on the mountain and burnt in such kilns to reduce it to a powder. The powder was then used as a mortar for construction and it was also used to whitewash the houses.

Before making the final climb there is a second kiln on the left at the bend in the path.

The summit is marked by a metal sign and a triangulation point. However, it is not the highest point of the mountain. The triangulation point is at 980m (976m on the IGN map), but the highest point is half a kilometre to the north at 1007m. There is no path to it and to get there is a scramble through inhospitable terrain.

Below the triangulation point to the west is the village of **Acebuchal**. It is from this spot that the moriscos plunged to their deaths in 1569. To the north the high cone-shaped peak of Lucero (1775m) dominates; across the valley the flat-topped mountain is La Cadena. Off to the south the view is over Frigiliana down to Nerja.

There is no other option but to return on the same path to Frigiliana. If you didn't spot the second lime kiln coming up it will be more obvious on the return journey. It can be seen as the path bends to the right at the foot of the first main descent. On the return you can see that Frigiliana is divided into two parts. The older part is nearest El Fuerte and the newer extension is furthest away. As the path approaches the base the river channel that carries water to the reservoir can be seen. This water has come from a dam on the Rio Higueron.

As you descend through the village it is worth examining some of the **ceramic plaques** on the walls. These were erected in the 1960s and tell the history of the village. Plaque No 3, at the bottom of Calle Amargura and the top of Calle Hernando El Darra reads:

Plaque No 3

'Andrés el Chorairán, native monfi from Sedella, encouraged the spirits of his people to bring them to rebellion. The young people who started to agitate were refrained by the Moor, Luis Méndez, an influential man in Canillas, but he couldn't stop them attacking the inn of a Christian, and killing several people in it. The judge of Vélez, Pedro Guerra, came along and many innocent Moors, among them, Luis Méndez, who had stopped the revolt, were imprisoned and burdened with chains, and subjected to cruel torture.'

The main street of the Calle Real winds its way past the town hall to the church.

Part of the **Iglesia San Antonio de Padua** dates as far back as the period of the morisco rebellion. It is a quaint old church and well worth a visit. In front of the church there is a square with a restaurant.

EXTENSION TO NERJA

Walking back to Nerja will take from 1½ to 2 hours. It can be done via the gorge of the Rio Higueron (see Walk 3) or returning by road and taking the obvious detour before a small restaurant above the Higueron river bed.

WALK 3
La Cruz del Pinto

Start/Finish	car park at the end of Calle Puente Viejo, the street just off the first roundabout at the (lower) entrance to the town (beyond Parque Verano Azul)
Alt Start/Finish	if passable, about a kilometre further up the river bank (drive up through town, turn down Calle Picasso and turn right at the end of the road to find somewhere to park)
Distance	12km or 9½ km by the high-level return route; 2km less from the alternative start point
Difficulty	2
Time	4½ hrs or 3½ hrs by the high-level return route; 30mins less from the alternative start point
Height gain	400m

A short climb to the nearest high viewpoint above Nerja, returning along the gorge of the Rio Higueron. Depending on the time of year, be prepared to get your feet wet in the river on the way back.

THE STORY OF LA CRUZ DEL PINTO

Francisco Pinto was a sea captain whose ship was in danger of sinking during a wild storm in the Mediterranean. Pinto went on his knees and gave a solemn undertaking that, if he and his crew were saved, he would erect a cross on the nearest mountain to where he would come ashore. He managed to drop anchor at Burriana Beach and soon afterwards erected the cross on this mountain. (Some would say that he cheated and that his cross should have been erected on El Cielo, a far more formidable task.)

Walk out of Nerja along the Chillar River under the motorway and up past the cement factory. Immediately after the cement factory, and before the quarry, there is a culvert over the river beside a tall gum tree. The walk crosses over this culvert to climb the concrete road and proceed between houses, ignoring all minor paths off it. The route contours around the mountain to climb it from the southwest.

At a crossroads there is a steep path down to the left and a concrete road up to the right, before the gates of, and running alongside, No 61. Walk up this road. ▸

Stay on the concrete road, passing all houses, to head out into the country. The road comes to a point where there is a Y in it, with two roads stretching off ahead (215:420785:4070634). Take the road on the right that goes up to Quinto Pino.

Walk up this road for a short distance until the road turns to the left and descends to the gates of Quinto Pino. There are signs on the right, one of them, a Parque Natural sign, is on the side of a track. There are cairns on either side of the track (210:420800:4070640). This is where the shorter version of the route returns. This track winds its way to the summit, a mere 20 minutes away.

There are a few steep steps over bare rock on the approach to the summit. The cross is set into a concrete block. Within the cross there is a tabernacle, which contains religious objects.

If you miss the turning, further along there is a dead-end lane and sign on the left, at No 19; turn right just after this crossroads to rejoin the walk, following a sign for a house called Quinto Pino.

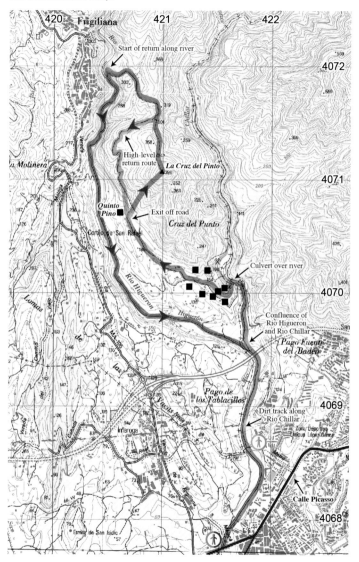

The path up to La Cruz del Pinto

From the El Pinto summit there are **fine views**, not only over Nerja and the coast, but also over west to Frigiliana and north to the Almijaras.

On the other side of the summit find the path going down towards Frigiliana. The track is a little steep in places. Eventually it arrives at a clearing where there are multiple paths. Take the path going down to the Rio Higueron.

Shorter high-level return route
The road on the immediate left at this junction is the shorter route option that returns hugging the side of the mountain. To follow this route, keep left at all junctions. The road passes above the Quinto Pino house, where it rejoins the outward route.

The walk back via the **Rio Higueron** is much more interesting than the flat return at high level. You will need to wade through the river, where water may be as much as ankle deep, but the experience is well worth it. ▸

There is a gorge en route that is similar to the Chillar gorge, but not as spectacular.

The path meanders from the left river bank to the river itself and out to the right bank. In places there are enormous **limestone boulders** in the river. Around the largest of them steps have been made.

Emerge eventually onto the gravel river plain and walk back out to the dirt track back to Nerja.

WALK 4
The Gorges of the Rio Chillar

Start/Finish	car park at the end of Calle Puente Viejo, the street just off the first roundabout at the (lower) entrance to the town (beyond Parque Verano Azul)
Alt Start/Finish	if passable, about a kilometre further up the river bank (drive up through town, turn down Calle Picasso and turn right at the end of the road to find somewhere to park)
Distance	15km or 13km from the alternative start point
Difficulty	3
Time	4hrs or 3½ hrs from the alternative start point
Height gain	400m
Options	You can go higher up to the dam at La Presa or up to the top of the ravine to walk its ridge, or just visit the gorge if you don't have time for the climb.
Note	This walk should not be done on a day when heavy rainfall is forecast. The water can rise suddenly after rain. Shorts are essential and some walkers go in swimsuits. Bring a towel if you want to take a dip.

If there is one walk that every visitor to Nerja should do then it's this one. After the Cave of Nerja the gorges are the second biggest tourist attraction here. You can touch the sides of these cliffs with each hand and yet they are so tall that the sky is shut out. During the summer they are crammed with people escaping the heat of the coast in the cool waters.

The route described here goes in the opposite direction to the route that most people follow, climbing up first to circle over the gorges and then descending to walk out along the river. This way feet stay dry until the final stages and legs don't get as wet when you are walking with, rather than against, the river's flow.

There are many access points to the river, the most obvious being from the car park at the end of Calle Puente Viejo and another to park along the river bank near Calle Picasso, subject to the state of the river bank and road.

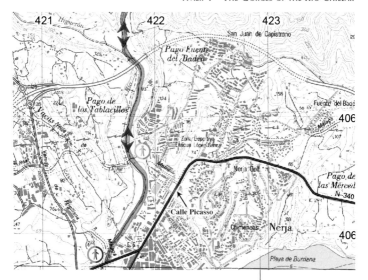

Walk along the bank of the Rio Chillar. You will pass a seven-storey block of flats on Calle Picasso that is built on the rock, with a cave underneath. As the road passes under the motorway you can also spot a white house perched high above, immediately under the carriageway. The front wall of the house hides a cave in the rock. Tall bamboos line the route at this point; later on, groves of avocados do so.

The walk passes a former quarry where pink limestone was once extracted. From here you need to pick your way along the river, crossing it many times on the stone dams, trying to stay dry. Two and a half kilometres beyond the motorway is the **electricity station**. The path turns off to the right fifty metres before you get to it. There is a circular red bricked structure in the river. Thirty metres beyond it on the right (and fifty metres short of the concrete ramp up to the generating station – at 135:421365:4071200) the climb begins up a gravel scree slope. The start of the route has been obliterated during recent construction work in the maintenance of the water

49

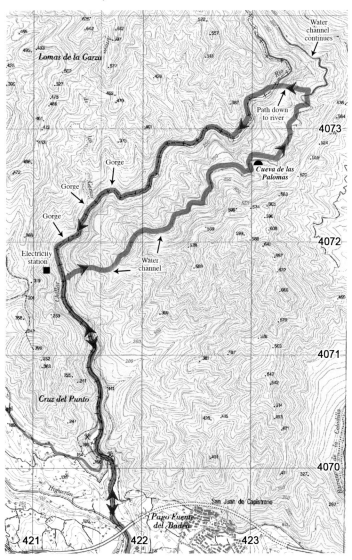

Wading through the gorges

channel. Above the scree slope the water channel has a cover and the path comes off this cover.

The path is steep and narrow. It joins concrete steps and rises again. For a section the walk is alongside a large diameter pipe, then it rises to the higher river channel. Now it follows the concrete river channel as it contours around the side of the ravine.

> This **water channel** is the water supply to Nerja. It comes from the dam higher up the river, generates electricity at the station and flows into the town. The channel is very popular with toads, which dive in and look up from the base.

The water channel goes through a high cave, Cueva de las Palomas, the Cave of the Doves. The concrete covering to the river channel continues to deteriorate and care is required. There are sections where it is necessary to walk along a narrow precipitous path.

Detour to the top of the ravine
About one hundred metres before the cave there is a cairn and a path that leads up to the crest of the ravine. This is an option that is well worth the effort but, if you lack the energy at this point, continue along the water channel.

Some walkers bring sandals to wade through the water, but others keep the ankle support and just get their boots and socks wet. There are many deep pools for a quick dip.

The channel will eventually arrive at a point where a path crosses it. Here, descend down into the river and turn left to head for the gorges and then retrace your outward route back towards town. ◄

> The **gorges**, *los cahorros* in Spanish, are in a series of three narrow passageways deep through the rock. The Spanish word *chillar* means 'scream' and it can be imagined how the water screams through these narrow chasms in flood conditions.
>
> At the electricity station and beyond it's easy to spot the water supply channel clinging to the ravine.

WALK 5

The El Cielo circuit

Start/Finish	road junction, 4km along the Pinarillo track
Distance	14km
Difficulty	8
Time	7hrs
Height gain	1260m
Getting there	From Nerja, follow signs to La Cueva de Nerja, and then turn northwards up the Pinarillo track, a dirt-track road that goes off to the left immediately before the car park for the cave. Park at the first major junction, a fork in the road with a sign offering choices of a recreation area to the left and a sendero to the right.
Warning	The approach to El Cielo is known to be a haunt for vipers, and the undergrowth is dense, so it would be wise to wear gaiters. There is no water source on the mountain.
Note	The Pinarillo track is (sometimes) closed to cars from June to October, which would add a further 8km to the walk.
Option	If you have two cars leave one of them a kilometre past the recreation area and take 2km of road-walking off the route.

This is one of the really great walks of the Almijaras. El Cielo (1508m), from which you can see the mountains of Navachica, Almendrón, Lucero and Maroma, is only 8km from Nerja and it looms majestically over the town. This walk is also an excellent introduction to many of the landmarks in the Almijaras: it follows the Pinarillo track, where many walks start, and visits the Barranco de los Cazadores. You're certain to spot those other local features – the cabras montés – too.

Set off towards the recreation area. Water bottles can be topped up at the El Pinarillo recreation area, a wooded picnic spot along the path. The walk direction initially is towards Fuente del Esparto.

The **Fuente del Esparto** is a well-known landmark in the area and it is worth a little diversion to see it. A kilometre beyond the recreation area the road takes a sharp left where it crosses the ravine. This ravine is the Barranco de los Cazadores (the ravine of the hunters). The fountain is half a kilometre up the road away from the ravine.

The view to Navachica

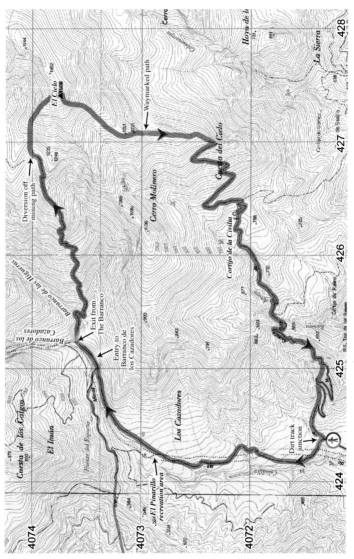

The El Cielo walk is into the ravine, walking over a dried river bed. Shortly, and fifty metres past a cave, there is a set of cairns and a path on the right (590: 425265:4073595). The narrow path beyond the cairns is a rather ill-defined path into Barranco de las Higueras. The path is tight and it is necessary to squeeze between rosemary, spiky furze and the occasional broom. **Do not** proceed into the depths of Barranco de las Higueras, but divert to the right – there is no other path. Ensuring you are on the path here is critical.

The path becomes quite steep, but it widens as it ascends. This is an old mining trail, its destination a disused mine on the side of El Cielo. The path eventually flattens as it approaches a two-pronged peak jutting up from the mountain. These are shown on the map at elevations of 1235m and 1248m. It is important to be careful here, for the old mining path begins to descend but the circuit leaves it, turning right.

From here to the summit the route is defined by little cairns. In this sparse vegetation the cairns at times compete for attention and on occasions are absent. However, the route is upwards towards the summit cross that should now be visible.

Eventually a short rock scramble is required to the summit.

When it was first erected, the galvanised **summit cross** had a full mirror on the side facing Nerja. The intention was that the sun would shine on it and reflect down into the town. It did just that, but, because it was erected upright the intended effect only occurred during a few winter days. Now the mirror is broken and there is no reflection at all.

From the summit it can be seen that El Cielo is not an isolated peak, but rather the shoulder of a mountain ridge that stretches up to Navachica. Down from Navachica on the other shoulder is Cerro Cisne, and in the middle, under Navachica, is Almendrón. Beyond Almendrón in the distance is the hump of Maroma.

The summit cross

In the springtime these giant asphodels abound

The descent is on the same side of the mountain as the ascent. If there are other climbers there it is most likely they came up from the southwest. This is your way down, via a cleft in the mountain with slippery scree that requires care. The direction is initially towards the west (almost in the direction of ascent), but the well-defined path swings to the south and is waymarked. The gradient is far gentler than the ascent, and circles another pair of peaks jutting from the mountain before reaching some zig-zags. You emerge from these by a collection of ruins of old and modern buildings.

This is **Cortijo de la Civilia**. Apparently an eccentric woman once lived here, going around in the clothes of a policeman.

From the cortijo the path becomes a dirt-track road. A few kilometres further down the road begins to zig-zag and it is possible to take shortcuts on a narrower path until you finally reach your parking place at the road junction.

Virtually all of the mountain of El Cielo is a **blue-grey limestone**. It is in massive formation and unweathered, in contrast to the rock on, say El Fuerte, which is white and friable. Along the approaches to El Cielo there are outcrops of limestone conglomerate, rocks much younger in geological age.

WALK 6

The tour of Almendrón

Start/Finish	El Pinarillo recreation area
Alt Start/ Finish	entrance to the Barranco de los Cazadores, 1½ km beyond the recreation area
Distance	13km or 11km from entrance to Barranco de los Cazadores
Difficulty	8½
Time	6hrs or 5hrs from entrance to Barranco de los Cazadores
Height gain	960m
Getting there	From Nerja, follow signs to La Cueva de Nerja, and then turn northwards up the Pinarillo track, a dirt-track road that goes off to the left immediately before the car park for the cave. Follow this to the recreation area. Either park here or, if your car is up to it, continue on the track another 2km to the entrance to Barranco de los Cazadores.
Options	The Pinarillo track is (sometimes) closed to cars from June to October, which would add a further 8km to the walk. A short detour can be made to the top of Tajo del Sol (1549m). You could do this walk in reverse and rise to Almendrón sooner.

Almendrón is the jagged peak that can be seen from Nerja. It is said that Almendrón has many faces and, indeed, the views from Frigiliana and from Cómpeta are starkly different. The mountain is named after the natural limestone feature on its flank – an almond (*almendro*)-shaped tower – that cannot be seen from the town. This walk does not climb to any summit but merely passes under its stark features through some of the most breath-taking mountain scenery in the Almijaras.

This is not a waymarked walk but it follows a well-worn path. The difficulty rating is high because it is arduous in places, requires careful manoeuvring over boulders and scree, and involves a little scrambling. The walk can be divided into four parts: two hours in the ravine until the turn is made up and out of it; one hour to the highest point of the walk; a further hour to make the traverse and have lunch; and another hour to descend.

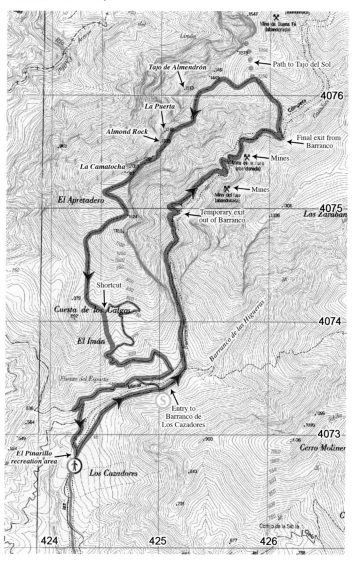

Tajo de Almendrón

Path to Tajo del Sol

4076

La Puerta

Almond Rock

Final exit from
Barranco

Mines

La Camatocha

Mines

El Apretadero

Temporary exit
out of Barranco

4075

Las Zaraban

Shortcut

Cuesta de los Galgos

4074

El Imán

Barranco de las Higueras

Fuente del Esparto

Minas

4073

Entry to
Barranco de
Los Cazadores

Cerro Moliner

El Pinarillo
recreation area

Los Cazadores

424   425   426

Walk up the dirt track heading northeast from the recreation area. After 1½ km the road turns sharp left over the ravine and the official route to Almendrón begins. There is a pumphouse and many gum trees here. Turn right off the road (continuing northeast) and into the ravine of the hunters, Barranco de los Cazadores.

The exit point from the ravine. Note the cairn on the right

> Within this quiet and sheltered canyon **plants** such as the Andalucían thistle flourish; the cade juniper (or prickly juniper) is also here, with its red/brown berries.

The walk into the ravine passes caves and meets a track on the left that also leads up to Fuente del Esparto. Further along there is an old lime kiln. The first 'step' is easy to scale. Ignore cairns inviting you to go right, and stay with the ravine.

> The ravine was once a significant **watercourse** and it is clear to see how rapid waters eroded the rock. There are many boulders, brought down by flood waters, that fill the canyon in places.

Within the Barranco de los Cazadores and above it there are numerous delicate **cade juniper** trees – *cade enebro* in Spanish. In the spring and summer they will have a profusion of little berries that gradually become brown and fall off in the autumn.

The path reaches a point where there has been a major rock slippage on the left and small cairns invite the walker to scale the scree. You could choose to follow these cairns, which lead along an old mining trail, or continue to follow the ravine – the latter is more standard and involves a little scrambling.

After perhaps an hour the ravine appears to come to a dead end and it is necessary to follow the small cairns up to the left and out of it. This is a steep climb that will circle to come back to the side of the ravine where a look back will show the enormous drop that you have avoided. At 1000:425725:4075535 the walk reaches the mines where the path is man-made. ◄

Look out for a holm oak on the right immediately after passing the first mine on the left.

Mining here was for **lead and galena** and the shafts are very deep.

The route soon turns back onto the former river bed, and about a kilometre along it is the critical turn. There is a large cairn in the bed of the ravine and another cairn on the left. The path out of the ravine almost doubles back here (1075:426150:4075650 – see photo).

There follows an hour of a strenuous climb with Tajo del Sol (1550m) on the right. Near the top there are multiple paths, but any of those going southwest will pass under Almendrón.

On the approach towards Tajo del Sol there is the option of taking the path to the right, which goes to the **top of Tajo del Sol** (the cliff of the sun). It is a one-hour diversion that is well worth the extra effort.

Care is required making the traverse under the cliffs of Almendrón, especially negotiating firstly the boulder

Andalucían thistle

ALMENDRÓN

The complex of Almendrón has five features:

- Tajo del Sol at 1550m
- Tajo de Almendrón (the cliff) at 1513m
- La Puerta – a gate/door in the ridge that connects Tajo de Almendrón to El Torre de Almendrón
- El Torre de Almendrón – the almond-shaped tower
- La Camatocha at 1312m – the beginning of the descent.

R to L (route order): Tajo de Almendrón, La Puerta, El Torre and La Camatocha with the trees on top

scree, then the stone scree. The path can be ill-defined in places.

> The energetic can deviate off the path and climb to the **top of Tajo de Almendrón**, but there is no clear track to it.

At the southwestern extremity of the traverse, past **Torre de Almendrón**, there is a crest that is the start of the descent. At this crest a climb up to **La Camatocha** will be rewarded with stunning views over the reverse side of the ridge and down the sheer drop into the Barranco de Almendrón.

The path down off La Camatocha is through rosemary and gorse that becomes more and more intrusive. The path passes through a gully at the base of a gorge. ◄

In the springtime tiny yellow flowers bloom here. They are miniature daffodils.

After half an hour or more below this pass the path emerges onto the end of a dirt-track road. You could follow this track all the way home but it is shorter to go right along a narrow track to descend, thus bypassing the lower road and emerging onto the same dirt-track further down.

Take the right options at junctions on the dirt track to reach the Barranco de los Cazadores and then turn right to the starting point (at the last T-junction there is the option to go left down into the Barranco de los Cazadores and follow back on the path you set out on).

The **Fuente del Esparto** is nearby and worth a visit. It involves a short detour along the dirt track to the right. There are lots of beehives around here and the bees tend to congregate around the fountain.

About 400 metres beyond the fountain there is a narrow path on the left that leads down and over the ravine and back to El Pinarillo.

THE CÓMPETA AREA

Sendero
Loma del Daire

Los Bojes →

Lucero from the return path (Walk 11)

Cómpeta is another of Andalucía's delightful white mountain villages. Clamped to the hillside, it is deep into the Almijaras and nestles under La Maroma. The town is 10 minutes down the motorway from Nerja and then 20 minutes of hairpin bends. Not a village that is vehicle-friendly, its narrow, steep streets wind up the hillside.

There are many walking opportunities from the village so you will see many other walkers with their boots and sticks. What is featured here is only a selection of the many walks in and around Cómpeta.

The first three of the walks can be combined together to make longer walks. From La Fabrica de la Luz Walk 7 goes to Puerto Blanquillo, and the following two walks, to Lucero and to Cerro la Chapa, start from Puerto Blanquillo.

WALK 7
La Fabrica de la Luz

Start/Finish	car park at La Fabrica de la Luz
Distance	11½ km
Difficulty	2
Time	4hrs
Height gain	500m
Getting there	Take the motorway and exit to Cómpeta, winding up the many hairpins to the village. Do not enter the village but bypass it in the direction of Canillas de Albaida. This is a mere two kilometres further on. On the approach to Canillas watch out for the sign – before you enter the village – for the recreation area of La Fabrica de la Luz and follow this peaceful country road for 3½ km to the car park.
Options	The walk can be combined with Walk 8 to Lucero or Walk 9 to La Chapa.

This is a gentle circular route along a river in a sheltered ravine through varied countryside, returning along a dirt track along the rim of the ravine.

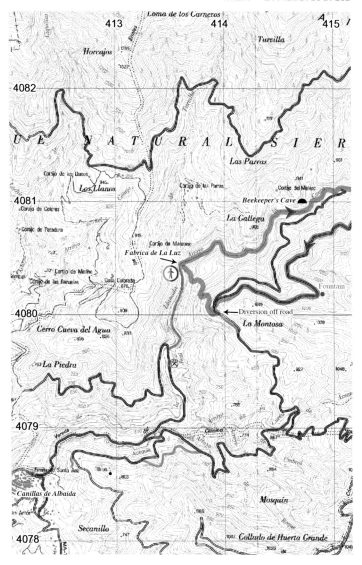

The village of Cómpeta with La Maroma in the background

La Fabrica de la Luz (the factory of light) is 3½ kilometres from Canillas de Albaida. It is a collection of old buildings, until the 1950s a hydro-electric generating station, from where several walks start. Camping was permitted here in 2013 (it had been forbidden up until then) and it is a popular spot for people to come and picnic on a Sunday.

At the parking area there is a dirt-track on the right. This will be the return route. Leaving the parking area under the buildings and beside the sign, take the path by the river that skirts a building, and follow this river, criss-crossing it many times, all the way to Puerto Blanquillo. The walk is waymarked. On the way it passes a large cave, Cueva del Melero (cave of the beekeeper), from which the ravine takes its name. Nowadays the cave is a shelter for farm animals.

It also passes three farmhouses (cortijos), **Cortijo del Melero**, **Cortijo de Moreno** and **Cortijo da Camacho**.

At one of the cortijos there is a grove of **Spanish chestnut trees**, the chestnuts of which are harvested in the autumn and brought down by mule.

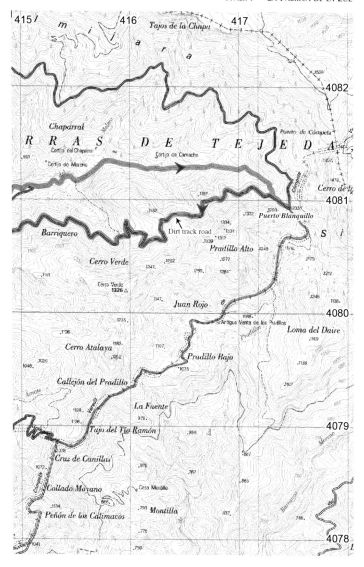

La Fabrica de la Luz

The path winds its way through a valley to rise up to a wide dirt-track road. Turning right on this dirt track is the return direction. But first turn left to go half a kilometre up to **Puerto Blanquillo**.

Puerto Blanquillo is a col at an elevation of over 1200m. The road passing over it eventually arrives back on the other side of Canillas de Albaida. Looking over the col the higher col of Puerto Cómpeta can be seen. Walks 8 and 9 use the dirt-track road to start from Puerto Blanquillo and proceed beyond Puerto Cómpeta.

The descent from Puerto Blanquillo is a long, but gradual one, almost 8km along the dirt track. After about 5km pass a **fountain** on the left (945:414820:4080160) where there should be a welcome supply of potable water. A kilometre after the fountain there is a dirt track on the right. This does not go back to La Fabrica de la Luz. A few metres further on take a path on the right marked with cairns (915:0413890:4080035). This steep path winds its way down to **La Fabrica de la Luz**. ◄

Continuing along the road takes you down to the road into La Fabrica de la Luz, but adds nearly four kilometres to the journey.

WALK 8
Lucero

Start/Finish	Puerto Blanquillo (1208m)
Distance	12km
Difficulty	5
Time	4½ hrs
Height gain	475m
Getting there	Drive to the village of Cómpeta. Do not enter the village but proceed in the direction of Canillas de Albaida. Follow the sign for the recreation area of La Fabrica de la Luz just before the village. After about 2km, just as the road enters the national park, take an unsignposted road to the right. At the first hairpin bend (after just a few hundred metres) take the dirt track road off this bend to the left at 750:0413800:4078800. (If you have to ask directions, ask for Puerto Blanquillo (blan-ki-yo).) After half an hour's drive over 10km of rough track, which must be taken slowly, the road eventually arrives at a bend at a col, where the rock is white.
Options	Can be combined with Walk 7 to make a 7–8hr round trip or Walk 9 to include an ascent of La Chapa.
Warning	This is a walk for a calm day with little wind. It is also not suitable for those who suffer from vertigo.
Note	On the 2008 Topografica Map there is a mistake: Lucero is shown as Cerro de los Moriscos and the nearby Cerro la Mota is shown as Lucero.

Of all of the mountains of the Axarquía the summit that is most impressive is Lucero. Climbing its precipitous path and arriving at the top of this inverted cone gives you a real sense of achievement as well as great views to the Sierra Nevada and down to the coast. It is one of the 'must do's in Andalucía.

There are several routes to get to Lucero, but there is only one path to the summit. What is featured here, in order to encourage anyone doubtful, is the simplest and easiest route. It involves a long drive over a rough dirt-track road to the base of the mountain so that the climb to the summit is then quite short and straightforward.

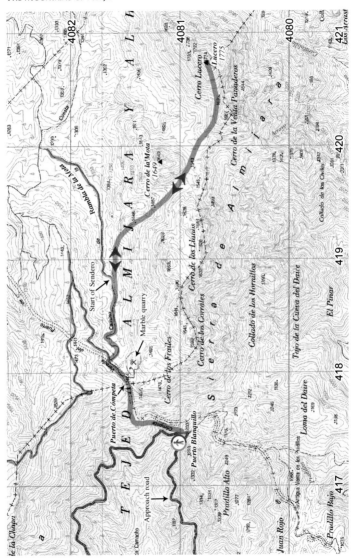

Above the col there is a view over and up to **Puerto Cómpeta**. To the left, looking directly north, it should be possible to pick out a waymark, a wooden stake directing you to climb the white rock. This is the path to be followed.

It leads up to a dense pine forest. **Be careful** This is a critical bit of route-finding. Count the waymarks from Puerto Blanquillo. Count the first one as the one that is just above the col. At the third one, just as the path enters the forest, do not follow the forest path, but swing to the right (see photo - the pine needles obscure the path). In 2011 there were lots of logs here. There should be some small cairns to mark this junction. ▶

The trail skirts the forest passing at the base of a firebreak and over to Puerto Cómpeta, with great views to the north and south. There is an enormous **quarry** here.

> **Cantera de Mármol** (the marble quarry), also known as Cantera del Macho, was a thriving place until 2010, when Andalucía's construction industry no longer needed stone. This may change and the quarry be reactivated in the future.

Continuing on the waymarked path leads into the depths of the forest, until a sign is suddenly encountered 'Fin de Sendero' – end of the walk – in the middle of nowhere!

The critical turn before entering the forest

The walk does not go through the quarry, but rather takes the road down the hill. This road is Rambla de la Mota. After a kilometre and a half you will see the **signpost for the sendero** on the right. Sendero Raspón de los Moriscos (the rough path of the converted Moors) is the only path up Lucero. The sign tells us that it is 2hrs to the summit from here. There are waymarks all the way to the top.

The gradient is gentle and enters a valley to the north of the mountain. It is only when the path passes through this valley that Lucero itself comes into view.

The smaller pointed peak is **Lucerillo**. Lucero means bright star, and Lucerillo means bright little star. The col between the two is known as Coladero de los Mosquitos, but there are never likely to be any in this windy patch.

The approach path towards Coladero de los Mosquitos with Lucero on the left

The path to the summit is not demanding and there is no scrambling, but there is a sheer drop to one side of it.

At the summit there is a surprise – a ruined brick structure. This was a **military post** built during the Spanish Civil War by the Franco side where lookouts had views in all directions, watching for any movements of Maquinadores (or 'plotters', generally shortened to Maqui), republican forces moving through the mountains. The view to the south, towards the sea, may be disappointing because the sun may be shining directly at Lucero. But it is possible to look over to the Sierra Nevada in the east and to La Maroma in the west.

The only option is to return via the path of ascent. Once again, care is required on this precipitous descent. ▸

At Puerto Cómpeta there is the option, for the very energetic, of ascending the firebreak and tackling Walk 9 to the summit of El Chapa.

WALK 9
Cerro de la Chapa

Start/Finish	Puerto Blanquillo (1208m)
Distance	9.5km
Difficulty	4
Time	4½ hrs
Height gain	630m
Getting there	Drive to the village of Cómpeta. Do not enter the village but proceed in the direction of Canillas de Albaida. Follow the sign for the recreation area of La Fabrica de la Luz just before the village. After about 2km, just as the road enters the national park, take an unsignposted road to the right. At the first hairpin bend (after just a few hundred metres) take the dirt track road off this bend to the left at 750:0413800:4078800. (If you have to ask directions, ask for Puerto Blanquillo (blan-ki-yo).) After half an hour's drive over 10km of rough track, which must be taken slowly, the road eventually arrives at a bend at a col, where the rock is white.
Options	This walk can be combined with Walk 7.

Looking up from Nerja at the conical summit of Lucero you can see a mountain tucked in behind it that appears to be lower than it and has a humped summit. This is Cerro de la Chapa. It is actually higher than Lucero but less exposed and a better choice for a windy day.

This is not a waymarked walk, but it's an easy walk through pine forests and open land on an almost continuous track.

At Puerto Blanquillo there is a waymark post on the northern side of the col. Follow the path that is marked by these posts for 600m over rocky ground, but do not follow them into the forest.

Immediately short of the pine forest there is a path junction where the right-hand option must be taken (see photo). The path is initially covered in pine needles and winds its way over rocky ground to Puerto Cómpeta (1400:0417885:4081465).

On the right is Cantera el Macho, a **marble quarry**. Do not descend to the quarry but turn north to ascend the open firebreak. This steep climb will emerge onto a dirt-track path where you turn left. This dirt track must be followed for 4km.

The track winds its way around two peaks that are known as Las Dos Hermanas, the two sisters, and when the track rounds the second one the goal comes into view. It is well marked by a steel cairn with an aerial. The path eventually breaks up and the final climb to the summit (1820:0417800:4083320) is over bare rock.

From the summit there is a very good view of Lucero and the path to its summit. **Cerro de la Chapa** is on a ridge that is over a kilometre long, with Cerro de las Majanos (1806m) at its northern extremity.

Retrace your steps back to find the dirt track and follow it down, eventually joining the firebreak down to Puerto Cómpeta and walking back to **Puerto Blanquillo** along the path.

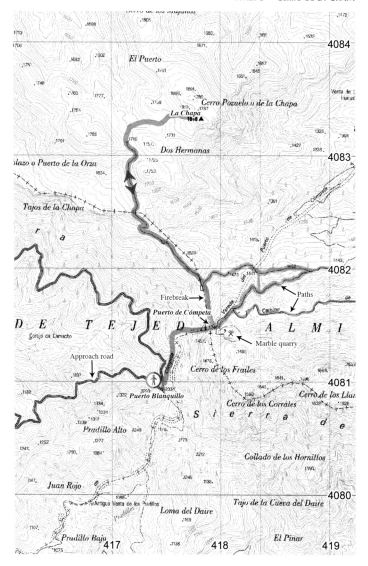

White marble and grey limestone from the El Macho quarry

Gentler option

For a gentler descent, stay on the dirt track when you reach the firebreak, walking east. At the first track junction (1465:0418700:408200), turn right and this path will come down to the base of the quarry. Climb back up the short distance to Puerto Cómpeta and retrace your steps to Puerto Blanquillo.

WALK 10
The oak forest of Salares

Start/Finish	Arab bridge, Salares
Distance	7km
Difficulty	3
Time	3½ hrs
Height gain	310m
Getting there	Get there either from Vélez-Málaga via Canillas de Aceituno or up from Algarrobo and Sayalonga. Just southeast of Sedella, Salares is in two parts and there is no vehicular access between them. The walk starts on the lower section, where there is a fine car park. Unfortunately there are no signs, so it may be necessary to ask 'Dondé esta el sendero para Puente Árabe?' or 'Where is the walk over the Arab Bridge?'
Options	The latter section of the walk is through housing areas and is not as interesting as the early section, so you could opt to retrace your steps back from Casa de Jaro instead.

This sheltered and undulating walk can be enjoyed whatever the weather. It leads from a tiny but delightful village through orange and olive groves and oak woodland to a viewpoint at over 900m. The route is waymarked but the waymarks are not always very regular. Expect to meet nobody for the first hour.

Salares (sal in Spanish means salt) gets its name from being the centre for the distribution of salt that was brought up from the coast. It is the smallest village in the Axarquía. With a dwindling population (it boasted 600+ souls in 1990 and was down to 250 in 2012) there is very little employment and many empty houses.

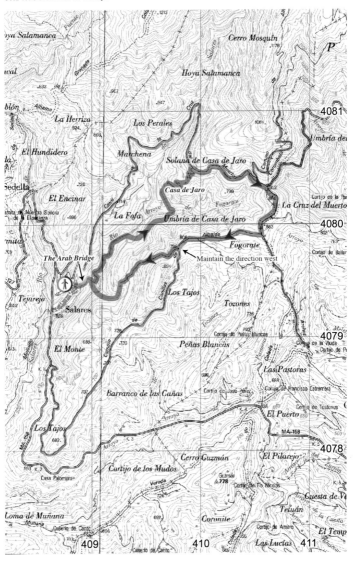

WALK 10 – THE OAK FOREST OF SALARES

Salares' most important tourist attractions are its minaret and Moorish bridge. The minaret is also Moorish, in the Mudejar style, with an intricate lace relief on each face.

In the smallest village of the Axarquía it should not be difficult to find the Arab bridge. ▶ Just over the bridge is the start of the walk. The sign tells us that it is 6.1km and will take three hours. Some would say it's a bit further than that and the time is a bit optimistic, too.

Through groves of orange, almond and olive trees, the walk follows a narrow path that rises and falls as it travels through the Arroyo de Fogarate. Before long you arrive in an oak woodland.

Although some guides refer to it as a Roman bridge it is known locally as the bridge of the Arabs.

This particular species of **oak** differs from the northern European oaks in that they do not grow to a significant height; the grain on their bark is tighter; the leaves are tiny and the sides of the leaves are not curved; but there is no mistaking the acorns.

The bridge of the Arabs

There are fine views back to the village along the trail. Follow the path down to cross the river and climb steeply up to Casa de Jaro, now just a collection of old ruins on a plateau overlooking the valley. The trail circles up over them and rises up to meet a dirt-track road. The hard climb is now over and the remainder of the walk contours around the ridge before descending.

La Cruz del Muerto (the cross of the dead man) is the area at the top of the walk, but the skyline is dominated by a modern villa, apparently unperturbed by the name.

You will need to pay close attention to follow the waymarks here – they are very infrequent – and make sure not to miss the turning off the road when it comes (800:409780:4079770). If you ask a local, they may direct you along the road, which is much longer than the waymarked path.

Apart from views over to Canillas de Albaida and Cómpeta there is little of interest on the last section of the walk. The southern-facing hills here are planted with vines and these vineyards are interspersed between modern, isolated villas. Eventually the path returns back into the village.

WALK 11
Cómpeta to Los Pradillos

Start/Finish	about 1km outside Cómpeta, off the road to Casa de la Mina
Distance	15km
Difficulty	3
Time	5–6hrs
Height gain	850m
Getting there	Drive to Cómpeta but do not enter the village. On the right, immediately before the viewing point over the village, follow the turning signed for the sendero and for Hotel Casa de la Mina. Although both take the same initial direction the goal is the sendero and not the hotel. It is necessary to turn off the steep concrete road for the start of the walk well before the hotel and pass the front door of a private house just before the walk's signboard. Parking at the start of the walk is a little scarce, and it may be necessary to retreat for a parking place.
Options	If you have two cars and can leave one at Casa de la Mina the last climb can be avoided. There is a good restaurant here.
Note	It would be a mistake to go to Casa de la Mina and attempt to do this walk in reverse. The markers are not designed for this option.

This route is a walk back in time into wild valleys that once supported a community of mining people. The settlement was also used during the civil war when the Maquis hid here from Franco's forces.

This is an undulating walk over rough ground. Although the difficulty rating is low, stiff boots with ankle supports are recommended. The walk is waymarked and circular, but the waymarks, strangely enough, do not lead back to the starting point. The route is called 'Sendero Casa de la Mina' but it begins over half an hour from Casa de la Mina.

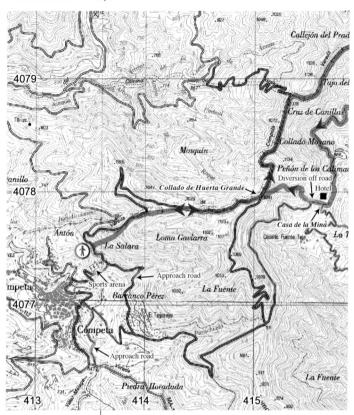

There are numerous paths and dirt tracks in these mountains and it is important to watch out for the markers and follow them. You will be switching from wide dirt tracks to narrow paths and back again.

◀ From the roadside, follow the waymarks to climb high over the village on a rough, steep path, alternating from dirt track to narrow path. After 3km reach a **col**, where you leave the track for another narrow path, following waymarks. Pause here and get your bearings.

This is the col that has to be climbed up to on the return journey. This col is known as **El Collado de Huerta Grande**, the col of the big market garden. Some 200m below the col are buildings. The large

one with the rooflight is Hotel Casa de la Mina and to the right of it is Casa de la Mina. There is a narrow path that goes from the col down to between these buildings. This is your return route.

The view from El Collado de Huerta Grande. The hotel is on the left. Casa de la Mina is on the right

Follow the trail along a dirt track through pines and among low rosemary bushes. This is an area that is a popular habitat for the cabras montés and the amphitheatre is stunning.

After a while reach another col where there is a path to the left that goes to Fabrica de la Luz. This is **Cruz de Canillas**, the cross of the taps. Fifty metres beyond this junction there is a ruin on the side of the trail. This is Ventorillos Dolores, the sorrowful little market.

After another few kilometres you reach your goal – the old settlement of **Los Pradillos**.

The first structure to be encountered in Los Pradillos is a **lime kiln**. The insides of the limestone walls would have been plastered in clay. Further up on the right are old **mine shafts**, now blocked.

Then the path comes to the main enclosure of Los Pradillos. It is on an elevated spot, with views down into the valley.

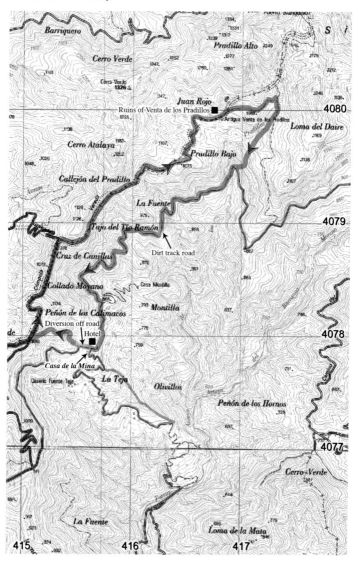

On the map it is marked as **Venta de Los Pradillos**, meaning the Inn of Little Pasture Lands. There were many inns along paths such as this to afford shelter to travellers.

On the north side of the walled enclosure there is an impressive circular flat area that would have had multiple uses: threshing, laying out *esparto* (coarse high grass) for weaving, as well as an ideal social and play area. Above the settlement is an extensive area of esparto used for making baskets, hats and ropes (maroma). Above the esparto fields there is yet another lime kiln, and further up there is yet another ruined building.

These mountains were popular hiding areas for the Maquis during the Civil War. Importantly, Los

Pradillos is not visible from the summit of Lucero. On that mountain there was a lookout constructed specifically to monitor the movement of the Maquis in the mountains.

The walk descends to cross a river bed. Do not follow the river bed but climb out on the other side. You will need to push through 2km of narrow track with the rosemary and gorse scraping your legs. The track eventually emerges onto a wide dirt track, which you follow around a hairpin bend. Looking back there is a fine vista of Lucero (the opening photo of this chapter) and you can just imagine Franco's men up there during the Civil War peering through their binoculars. This wide dirt track goes all the way back to the hotel. In the opposite direction the dirt track towards Lucero leads to Puerto Blanquillo.

After a long trudge, arrive at **Casa de la Mina**, the house of the mine. At the hotel a sign tells you that you have reached the end of the walk: if only that were true! There are, sadly, also no markers to direct you back to the start of the walk.

Pass the hotel and, at the first bend, where there are two electricity poles (one on each side of the road), take the rough path on the right. This leads to a narrower path that climbs up to the Collado de Huerta Grande. Once you reach the top, turn left and retrace your steps to the start of the walk.

THE VENTAS OF ANDALUCÍA

A venta is an inn or hostelry in Spanish. Throughout the country there were many positioned at strategic junctions of paths and these afforded shelter to the traveller. Of course, they also served as eating and drinking houses for the locals.

During the civil war the ventas in the countryside were seen by Franco as places frequented by the Maquis, and so he ordered for them to be destroyed. In 1940 many thousands of ventas, such as this one at Los Pradillos, were burnt to the ground.

LA MAROMA

Descending La Maroma (Walk 12)

La Maroma from Viñuela Lake

La Maroma is the highest of the mountains of the Axarquía, at 2069m. At the top its spine is flat – the section that is above 2000m is over a kilometre long and the section that is higher than 1900m is nearly four kilometres. There are four paths to the summit: from the southeast via Sedella, from the southwest via Canillas de Aceituno, from the west via Alcaucín and Alcazar, and finally from the northeast via Alcaicería and Cortijo Robledal. (There is a fifth route from the east, but this requires a four-wheel drive vehicle from Salares.) The routes are quite dissimilar, each with its own challenges and characteristics.

The name La Maroma refers to a rope made of reed/ rush, or in Spanish *esparto*. The esparto grows all over the region. It will be seen interspersed with the gorse, broom and rosemary or on its own in thick clumps. It is used for thatching and weaving baskets and hats. The long summit is Loma de Las Viboras, the spine of the vipers.

FOUR ROUTES TO THE SUMMIT

The option from Alcaicería-Robledal is the least onerous and the option from Sedella is at the limit of a day's hike. The Alcaucín-Alcazar route is not straightforward and it is easy to miss the shorter path. Although the physical task from Canillas de Aceituno is demanding, the round trip from Nerja is almost the same as via Alcaicería-Robledal. If it is the preference to get an early start on the climb

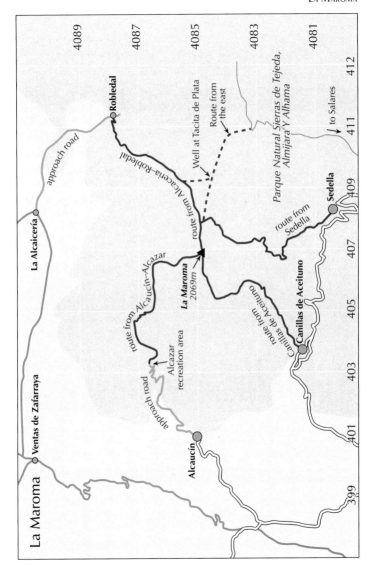

La Maroma

and devote time to the walk rather than time in a car then Canillas de Aceituno wins. However, there is a lot to be said for the spectacular drive through Ventas de Zafarraya and to experiencing the fertile plateau above it.

THE ROUTES AT A GLANCE					
Route	Elevation at start	Height gain	Distance	Time from Nerja*	Characteristics
Canillas de Aceituno	630m	1439m	19km	9hrs	Straightforward climb starting in the village. Waymarked. Plenty of interest en route. Easy access to start – 45mins from Nerja. Good water source.
Alcaucín/ Alcazar	850m	1219m	15km	8½ hrs	The waymarked path is 6km longer, and the shorter path is a little tricky. Doubtful water source. Easy access to start – 1hr from Nerja.
Sedella	588m	1481m	22km	10hrs	A long tedious path, steep initially, then gentle, and then steep again. Parking not always easy. Waymarked. Long drive to Sedella. Vulture sanctuary and old mill en route. One water source low down.
Alcaicería/ Robledal	1100m	969m	15km	8½ hrs	Consistently gentle gradient all the way. Waymarked. Path can be frozen in the winter. Long drive via Ventas de Zafarraya – 1hr 40mins. Water source (deviation)

* includes driving time from Nerja to the start of the walk

A WORD OF CAUTION

Whichever route is taken up La Maroma, vigilance at the summit is required to remember the direction of approach. When mist envelopes the summit it is very easy to become disorientated. Over the bare summit rock there are no paths and waymarks are scarce.

WALK 12
La Maroma from Canillas de Aceituno

Start/Finish	Canillas de Aceituno
Distance	19km
Difficulty	7
Time	7½ hrs
Height gain	1439m
Getting there	Drive to the village of Canillas de Aceituno. At the first roundabout instead of taking the main road into the village take the road to the left of it. There is a municipal car park just after you cross the bridge. Note that the car park is used as a market on Friday mornings, so you may have to find a space elsewhere.
Options	With two cars you could leave one at the visitor centre in Sedella and return along the route of Walk 14.

This walk starts from the historic and attractive village of Canillas de Aceituno and visits the old Moorish settlement of La Rabita before climbing to the prominent domed summit. The ascent is long but straightforward, waymarked all the way and has plenty of interest en route.

CANILLAS DE ACEITUNO

The direct translation of Canillas de Aceituno is the 'taps of the olive', but this is not the origin of the name. From ancient Arabic 'canillas' was a place where cane grew, and 'aceituno' has been distorted from the Arabic for silk. The village has a fine Roman bridge and an interesting cave, Cueva Fagara, where Neolithic remains were found. To sense the history of the village a visit should be made to La Sociedad, the first place where a workers' cooperative was established, and now a restaurant popular with the locals.

From the car park walk up a steep stone ramp that leads to a series of steps. At the top turn right and follow further

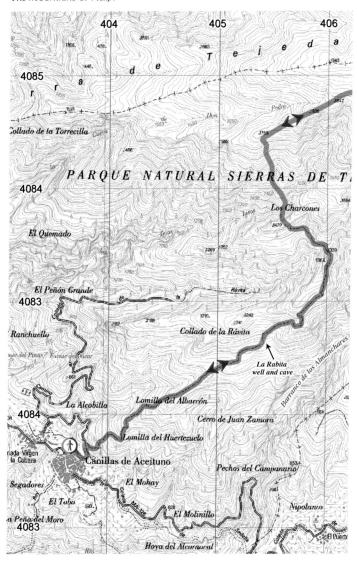

steps, all the time heading in the same northeasterly direction. There are multiple choices, but rest assured that they all eventually get to the start of the walk. There are steps en route that have a wooden handrail on the side.

Follow the sign for a sendero to 'Casa de la Nieve' (the house of snow). This is the local name for the summit of La Maroma and it originated from the custom to store snow and ice in a cave on the summit. The first sign suggests that the walk is only 6km, but the sign further up is more correct at 9km. Remember that this is the distance to the summit of La Maroma and does not include the return.

The ascent, with Canillas de Aceituno below

> This is a **waymarked path** all the way to the summit. The moderate gradient winds through pines and esparto over micaceous (green) shale in between outcrops of limestone.

After 45mins the path reaches the old settlement of **La Rabita**. ▸ Further along the trail there is a cave, and from the cave the ruins of old buildings can be seen.

There is a well here that has good water in it.

The flat summit of La Maroma with Sierra Nevada in the distance

A sign near the cave tells walkers that **La Rabita** was frequented by the Romans (100BC to 300AD). Later it was settled by the Moors (700AD), when there was a working mine here. The area later features in the annals of the morisco (converted Muslim) rebellion and punishment (1560). The water from the well was once piped to Canillas de Aceituno and you will have wandered over old ceramic pipes en route. In the springtime the stone trough below the well will be teeming with tadpoles.

Droppings on the path indicate that the cabras montés graze here.

From an elevation of approximately 1200m the enormous hump of La Maroma fills the vista. However, there is no need to be alarmed – the route does not head straight up its vertical face, but circles to the north to approach the summit from the west. ◄

The **path that crosses the Barranco de los Almanchares** can clearly be seen on the right. This path descends to the road between Canillas de Aceituno and Sedella.

At about 1300m the path passes to the right of the ruins of an old stone beehive refugio, and further up there is a smaller refugio below the trail on the right. There is a well at **Los Charcones**, but the flow out of it is very poor and therefore suspect.

The trail zig-zags out to the west and, when it eventually makes the turn to the east, is at an elevation of 1700m with only a little over 300m and a relatively flat 2km to go to the summit of **La Maroma**.

Coming down from the summit on this path poses few dangers and there are no particularly steep sections. The route is obvious almost all the way. However, upon arrival at the outskirts of the village there is no clear path to the car park. If you can't remember exactly how to get to the critical steps, don't worry too much – walking through private property is something the locals are used to and they are very friendly about it.

WALK 13

La Maroma from Alcaucín

Start/Finish	Alcazar recreation area
Distance	15km
Difficulty	8
Time	6½ hrs
Height gain	1219m
Getting there	Alcaucín is off the road from Vélez-Málaga going north. Pass the signposts for Viñuela and later take the road to the right. Just as it enters the village there is a road to the left signposted for the recreation area of Alcazar, 5km along a dirt-track road. At Alcazar there is a spacious car park and a sign describing the walk.
Options	Follow the waymarked longer version of the route for a gentler gradient but a round-trip distance of 21km.

The Alcazar recreation area is a popular area for school outings and for picnics. The route described here shortcuts the waymarked path that is used by loggers and known as Castillones. The shortcut saves 6km in total but it is steeper and not as well defined.

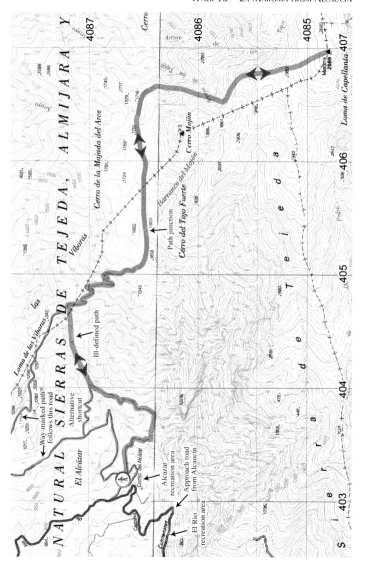

Attention to the route is essential in the initial stage as this path breaks into several paths and all but one go nowhere.

Walk up the stone steps from the car park and go through the picnic area, up alongside a fast-flowing water channel, to a wide track with waymarks. The waymarked, longer walk starts where there is a chain over the road then it swings left. Follow this just to the first junction (850:403250:4086640) where, just beside a waymark, a path goes off to the right. Take this path. ◄

When you arrive at a grove of tall pines (critical point) be sure to walk up through them – do not cross the stream – although the pine needles will obscure the

Dolomitic limestone en route to the summit

path. At the end of the grove of pines there is a slippery rock to climb and then the route follows the path above it that crosses the same stream. The climb now is steep as it proceeds up the Barranco de Higuera in a direction east to northeast. It joins a wider path for a short distance and then traverses over a firebreak and climbs along a crest, following little cairns, until it reaches the waymarked Castillones route at a galvanised rain funnel.

This place is the **Loma de las Viboras**, the spine of the vipers (perhaps gaiters would be advisable!). Below and to the west the waymarked road can be seen. Turn right and climb the clear zig-zag path, following the waymarks.

At **1650m** the path arrives at another rain funnel where there are multiple paths. ▶ The waymarked path passes a well, Fuente del Espino, but the water in it is rather suspect. The trail circles around **Cerro Mojón** to swing in a southerly direction to the summit.

> The **limestone** here is friable and weathered and there are places to rest in the shade and out of the wind.

From Cerro Mojón to the **summit triangulation point** is two, relatively flat, kilometres. On the way over to the summit, which is reminiscent of the Burren in County Clare in Ireland, cross a karst limestone pavement, with holes and caverns in it formed by mildly acidic waters reacting with and dissolving the limestone.

The return to Alcazar is not as complicated as the ascent. It is easier to notice the vagaries of the path and to compare the waymarked path and the shorter route in this direction.

A second shortcut can be taken by coming off track and trudging up the Barranco del Mojón, but this only curtails the journey by half a kilometre each way.

The little summit marker sign

WALK 14

La Maroma from Sedella

Start/Finish	Sedella
Distance	22km
Difficulty	8½
Time	8½ hrs
Height gain	1481m
Getting there	It takes about the same time to get to Sedella by travelling via Algarrobo-Sayalonga as it does via Vélez-Málaga-Canillas de Aceituno. The latter is longer but involves fewer twisting roads. Upon entering the village of Sedella there is a large sign on the left for the visitor centre. Find a place to park and head to this building.

This walk starts in the quaint little village of Sedella, which has plenty of attractions of its own. The route was only waymarked in 2011 and is strenuous and very steep in places. It is important to be prepared, pick a day with fine weather and start early, particularly if you plan to visit the vulture sanctuary on the way.

The former route up to La Maroma from Sedella, with a start west of the village, is a little longer and more gradual and heads off northeast initially. That alternative, via Cortigo de la Herreriza, follows the ancient path between Sedella and Alhama.

A WORD OF CAUTION: LEAVING ALCAUCÍN

Before leaving Alcaucín at the end of your walk note that at the first road junction you have a choice between Viñuela-Vélez-Málaga to the left or Granada to the right. The left option follows a narrow, twisting road for many kilometres. For the most direct route to the coast go right towards Granada. The road comes to the main road where there is a left turn back to Vélez-Málaga via the main road.

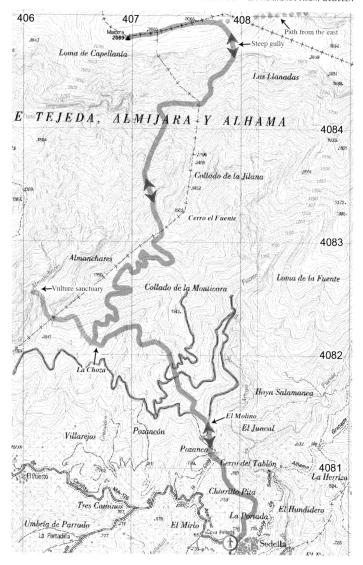

The **visitor centre** in Sedella, which is dedicated to the mountain environment, was opened in 2011 and has many interactive displays. Off season it is only open at weekends. The receptionist can help with directions and information.

From the visitor centre the route is up the main street of the village (quite narrow) to a bar. Here turn left, following the signs. The path is initially quite steep as it climbs up to a large, white building facing south, with a water channel on its right-hand side. This is **El Molino**, an old flour mill that was powered by water. Under the archway the old timber workings can be inspected. Outside there is a tap with potable water.

The trail passes in front of the building and then circles around above it, so that it is possible to look into the old reservoir that once serviced it. Climb up the path and pass two flat-roofed concrete structures on the right. A little further on, reach a small, thatched refugio. This is **La Choza**, a former lookout hut.

The thatched refugio

From La Choza the **vulture sanctuary** (Buitrera) is less than a kilometre away but there is little point in making the detour if you don't have binoculars.

Extension to the vulture sanctuary
To get to the vulture sanctuary turn left. There is a thatched hide where the vultures can be watched across the valley. Within a fenced enclosure animal carcasses are left for the birds to feed on. Often there are injured birds there. The small building is a shelter for the birds and their nests. The signs are quite clear to get back to the main track and turn left to resume the climb.

A Griffon vulture

For the main route, the trail up is around to the right from La Choza and now follows established, graded dirt tracks, which are rather long and tedious. You may decide to take shortcuts through the switchbacks on the return journey. Above the open pavement area known as Era the trail narrows to a path and becomes steeper. Ahead there is an escarpment protruding from the mountain called **Cerro el Fuente** (The Mountain of the Water Source). The path passes under it (it is at 1504m) and the elevation is 1300m, so you are almost halfway up. ▶

En route there is a doubtful water source at an elevation of 1350m.

The path arrives on the spine of Maroma via a steep gully and it is important to memorise the features of this junction for the descent. Turn left for the summit (or right, if you need water, for Tacita de Plata, where there is a pipe emerging from the rock with a constant flow of good water into a stone trough).

> The **summit** of Maroma is a long plateau, over four kilometres in length. Its karst surface has many crevices, some quite enormous. The largest of the sinkholes, Sima de Nieve, is all of 54m in depth, and is so called because it fills with snow in the winter and was used, for several months into the spring and summer, as a source of ice.

There is no other option, if your transport is at Sedella, but to retrace your steps. Care is required on

Signpost en route

those steep sections, but the tedious switchbacks can be cut through.

If you have made good progress and time is available, it would be worth visiting the fine Roman bridge on the northeast side of the village. Unfortunately it entails returning to Sedella and climbing again. It is northeast of the village (shown on the Topografica map).

WALK 15

La Maroma from La Alcaicería

Start/Finish	Robledal
Distance	15km
Difficulty	6
Time	5hrs
Height gain	969m
Getting there	Come off the motorway at Vélez-Málaga and head north in the direction of Alhama de Granada and Zafarraya. The road steepens and passes through a natural pass in the Sierra Tejeda – Ventas de Zafarraya. After 10km from Zafarraya, the road arrives at La Alcaicería. There is a hotel on the road facing the approach. Take the dirt track to the right of it in the direction of Cortijo de Robledal. Ignoring all junctions on the road, after 6km the road reaches the ruin of Robledal and a sign indicates the route. There are plenty of places to park in the shade.
Note	Because this approach is from the north, ice and snow may linger on the path in spring and in very cold conditions crampons may be required. If you are using the 1:25,000 maps you will need four of them to cover this route.

This is a waymarked trail, with a consistently gentle gradient, all the way to the summit of La Maroma. The long drive in via Ventas de Zafarraya compensates with spectacular views and a good place to eat at Alcaicería on the way back.

Follow the waymarks from the sign at the car park. The route is initially through a pine forest on a gentle gradient passing through Barranco del Selladero. It climbs steadily to a bend in the path with a sign pointing to **El Salto de Caballo** (the horse jump).

From here the trail rises to a junction at 1900m, where it passes a gully coming from the left. This is the

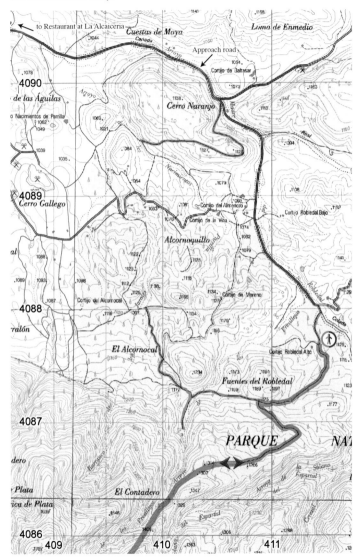

path from Sedella. ▶ Continue on to walk over the relatively flat two kilometres of stone pavement to the summit and the triangulation point.

The name of this area is Loma de Las Víboras (the spine of the vipers).

> The top of **La Maroma** contains many deep crevices and the path over the summit pavement is not defined, so care is required in cloudy conditions. The mountain can suddenly be engulfed with no return path in sight. When the summit is covered in snow there is the added danger of stepping into a hole.

Retrace your outward route back to **Robledal**.

Alternative descent
The well at **Tacita de Plata** is a worthwhile diversion on the descent. Proceed along the path over to the east to reach the well. Below it there is a sign for the alternative path to El Robledal.

View of La Maroma from Cortijo de Robledal

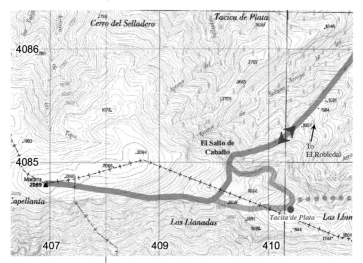

A pause for refreshments at the **Alcaicería Hotel** is highly recommended. This is a popular, inexpensive eating place. Outside of the summer months there will be a large fire blazing in the huge fireplace.

THE VALLEY OF
THE RIO VERDE

Hang-gliders taking off in the valley

The Rio Verde (Green River) flows south from the mountains to the sea at Almuñécar, and is the eastern extremity of the area covered in this guide. Three walks are featured in the valley: the first to the second-highest point of the Almijaras, Navachica, the second to a very pretty and unusual waterfall and finally a very brief walk to a mountain that stands off from the main cordillera, Lopera. Navachica is a long day's hike, but the other two can be combined into one day's excursion.

Otivar, another of the white villages of Andalucía, where there are popular restaurants with stunning views overlooking the valley, is well worth a visit. Above Otivar there is an area frequented by hang-gliders, where you can watch them taking off and landing.

WALK 16
Navachica

Start/Finish	Barranco de Cazadores or Campsite of Pinarillo
Distance	17km (18km via Tajo del Sol)
Difficulty	7 (10 for Optional Descent via Tajo del Sol)
Time	7½ hours (8½ hours descending via Tajo del Sol)
Height Gain	1283m
Getting There	From Nerja follow the signs to La Cueva de Nerja and then turn left and northwards, just before the parking area for the cave along the dirt track road to the Pinarillo Recreation Area. Go past the recreation area for another 2 km until the track turns sharp left. This is the entrance to the Barranco de Cazadores (the ravine of the hunters). Park here and walk into the barranco.
Options	Getting to the summit of Navachica may be quite sufficient for most people as a one-day expedition. However, for the adventurous, there is the option of descending via Tajo del Sol. The descent is precipitous and requires very careful attention to cairns and markers. It involves scrambling down a sheer cliff face.

In the first printing of this book the walk to Navachica was from Peña Escrita in the Valley of the Rio Verde. However, the zoo at the start was closed in 2016 and this is a replacement walk.

At 1832m Navachica is the highest point in the Sierra Almijara and the second highest point in the region covered by this guide. It dominates the eastern end of the mountains of Nerja, vying with La Maroma in the west, and it is the nearest of the mountains to the Sierra Nevada. (A navachica is a special knife for opening shellfish, but it is unlikely that this word has anything to do with the mountain's name).

Lying many kilometres from any main road its remoteness means that few walkers ever visit its summit.

This is not a way-marked trail, so it is essential to take care with the directions, to follow the various cairns and paint marks and to remember the way back. There is no scrambling involved, but there are parts of the trek that are steep.

Start at the entrance to the **Barranco de Cazadores** (548:424970:4073250), (the same start as Walks 5 and 6), proceeding into the barranco and following it north-eastwards. The route is all the way through this ravine up to its end. Become acquainted with the cairns and paint

The summit of Navachica

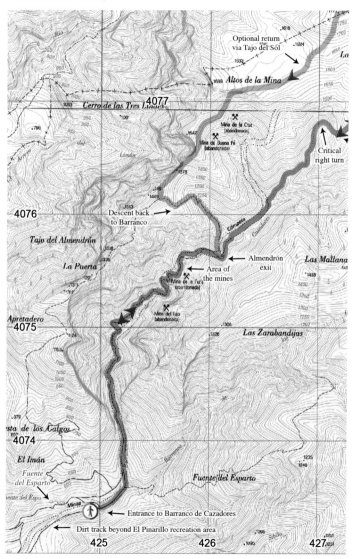

Optional return
via Tajo del Sol

Altos de la Mina

Critical
right turn

Cerro de las Tres Linares

4077

Mina de la Cruz
(abandonada)

Mina de Buena Fé
(abandonada)

Descent back
to Barranco

4076

Cómpeta

Tajo del Almendrón

La Puerta

Almendrón
exit

Las Mallana

Area of
the mines

Mina de la Fura
(abandonada)

Mina del Tajo
(abandonada)

Apretadero
4075

Las Zarabandijas

esta de los Galgos

4074

El Imán

Fuente
del Esparto

Fuente del Esparto

Minas

Entrance to Barranco de Cazadores

Dirt track beyond El Pinarillo recreation area

425   426   427

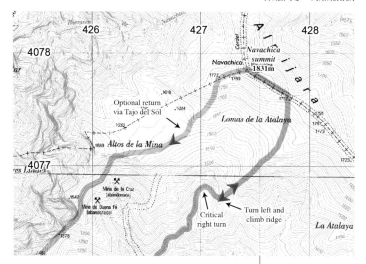

marks that guide you along the path. After some kilometres the marks direct you out of the barranco, climbing steeply to join an old mining trail. This well preserved path passes several mines, the first on the left and the last at the end of a descent.

If you turn back to the right into the valley at the last of the mines and walk back you will find a cave on the left near a large boulder. This cave (a former mine) is now the home of a small colony of bats.

The trail continues and returns to the ravine (barranco) eventually passing the exit on the left to **Almendrón**. After some kilometres the trail rises steeply initially over bare limestone then through stony inclines. There is a critical turn to the right to be made at 1365:427030:4076820. This should be quite clear

Bats in the old mine under Almendrón

113

from the markers, but it is important not to miss it, for to proceed straight would be over very steep ground. A few metres further the trail reaches the **Navachica ridge** where there is a welcome rest area. The direction is now to turn left towards the **summit**.

The approach to the peak is over bare rock where the markers are not easy to see, so take care to remember the way back. At the summit, marked by a concrete plinth, there will be the clearest view from the Mountains of Nerja to the snow-capped Sierra Nevada. It is also now possible to look at the two ridges that project out like arms from Navachica, one over to Almendrón and the other towards El Cielo. The double hump of Cisne, not visible from Nerja or many other places, is clear here.

The safest route back is to return by the ascent route, taking care on the sections of steep, stony paths.

The alternative descent is via **Tajo del Sol** and over to Almendrón, an alternative that is not for the faint-hearted and involves good navigation skills and great care over bare rock.

There is no distinct path from Navachica over to Almendrón, so that it is necessary to find a way to descend down and along the ridge. On the approach to Tajo del Sol cairns mark the only viable path, and it is essential to find these cairns. Now the trail descends down the cliff face of Tajo del Sol (the cliff of the sun), zig-zagging on the descent. When it reaches level ground again there are a few kilometres of walking until it reaches the paths of Almendrón.

There are two choices here: proceed straight under Almendrón or turn left. If it is intended to walk over and under Almendrón, then it would be wise to read about it in Walk 6. This option involves some scrambling over scree and boulders, to pass by **Torre de Almendrón**, the rock that is shaped like an almond.

The shorter option is to turn left upon meeting the Almendrón paths, at 1386:425486:4075943, and descend back into the barranco.

WALK 17
The Petrified Waterfall

Start/Finish	on the A4050, 4km north of El Mirador de la Cabra Montés
Distance	10km
Difficulty	3
Time	3hrs
Height gain	300m
Getting there	From Almuñécar you need the road to Jete ('Hetay') and Otivar, which is in the opposite direction to the beach. Avoid coming into town from the south and come in near the centre of town. Follow the traffic around to the right and take the road north that passes under the A340. Drive north through Jete and Otivar to pass the buildings on the left that make up Mirador de la Cabra Montés. Less than two kilometres from the Mirador there is a road to the left with the large entrance sign for the Sierras Tejeda, Almijara y Alhama. The dirt track on the left descends to the waterfall from here but the waymarked walk leaves the main road another 2km further on, where there is limited space to park.
Options	This walk and Walk 18 to the summit of Lopera can be combined into one day.

This short route takes you on an adventure into the secluded valley of the Rio Verde to visit a very pretty and unusual waterfall.

This walk descends, very steeply in places, from the main road down to the waterfall and returns along a dirt track back to the main road. There are no waymarks on the return route.

If you only want to see the waterfall you would be better doing the route in reverse, driving off the main road down to a barrier and then following the dirt track to the river and the waterfall. This option is not waymarked at all.

Take the narrow waymarked path down from the main road on an undulating course around the mountain of

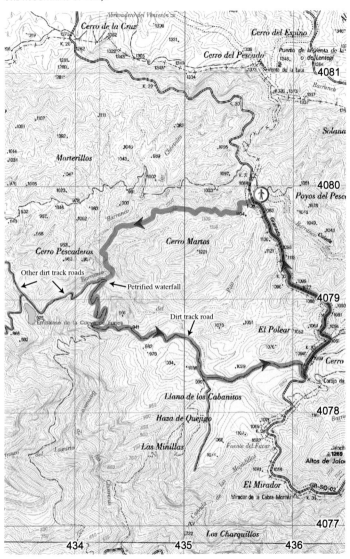

The petrified waterfall

Cerro Martos. Very soon you are deep into the wilderness of the Valley of the Rio Verde, walking through pines and stunted junipers. The jagged columns of white limestone dominate the landscape.

In less than an hour make a steep descent, aided by ropes in places and handrails over concreted steps elsewhere. Before reaching the bottom you will be able to hear the waterfall and then catch your first glimpse of it. ▸

At the base of the waterfall, in the shade of the trees, there is a lovely pool with cool water. It is an ideal spot to have a picnic.

The **waterfall** was created by the trunks of trees becoming engulfed in the lime chemicals of the water. About 20 years ago the tree trunks had been

117

Detail of the waterfall

felled and were being brought down the river. They were manoeuvred over the waterfall and left to stand there. Over the years the lime minerals in the water covered the trunks and formed a thick coating.

Leaving the waterfall the path comes to a junction of two dirt-track roads. Take the road on the left that rises to the south. The road to the west follows the Rio Verde and goes deeper into the valley.

There are no waymarks to follow, but the route is quite straightforward. The dirt-track road gradually rises on a three-kilometre trek up to the main road, from where there is a relatively flat further three kilometres back along the road to the start of the walk.

WALK 18

Lopera

Start/Finish	on the A4050, 6km north of El Mirador de la Cabra Montés
Distance	8km
Difficulty	1
Time	3hrs
Height gain	250m
Getting there	From Almuñécar you need the road to Jete ('Hetay') and Otivar, which is in the opposite direction to the beach. Avoid coming into town from the south and come in near the centre of town. Follow the traffic around to the right and take the road north that passes under the A340. Drive north through Jete and Otivar to pass the buildings on the left that make up Mirador de la Cabra Montés. The start of the walk is 6km beyond the mirador. On the left of the road is the signpost for the walk and there are parking spaces opposite.
Options	This walk and Walk 17 could be combined into a single day.

It is a rarity to be able to walk for just an hour and reach the summit of the highest mountain in an area to experience its 360-degree vista. But you can with Lopera (1485m) and the ascent is easy.

It is also rare to be able to walk in Spain through meadows and wheat fields, passing hawthorn and deciduous oak trees, with grasses and flowers that would be common in Ireland and the British Isles.

It is less than 3km from the main road to the summit of Lopera. Substantially the path is over a wide firebreak. For the entire approach the objective is clearly in view – a meteorological observatory perched on the summit. ▶

On the summit there is a fine **panoramic view**. To the east is the Sierra Nevada – Lopera is the

A third of the way up on the right you come to a prominent evergreen oak, but on the approach to the summit the trees are pines.

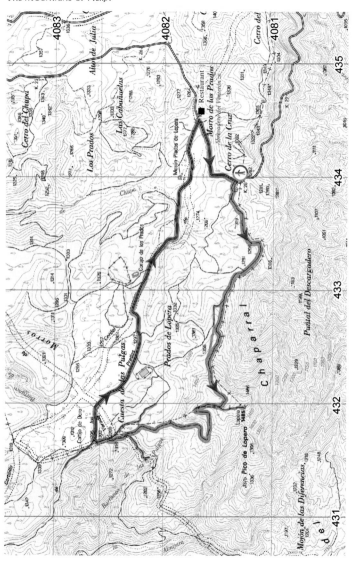

nearest summit in these mountains to the Sierra Nevada. The orientation table below the observatory picks out the other peaks to the south and west. Sadly there is no route from here to the summit of Navachica: the land between Lopera and Navachica is substantially in private ownership.

The waymarks only go to the summit of the mountain. The walk return is along unwaymarked dirt tracks. Walk away from the summit in a northerly direction, along a wide dirt track that descends directly north. Now the route is through pines on either side.

After 2km a road joins from the left and the signs indicate that the land to the left is private. So, continue northwards to a sharp bend in the road and where another path joins from the left. This is the area of the **Prados** (meadows) – fields that have been cultivated for grain for centuries. Follow the road to the right all the way down to the restaurant.

On the walk out there are hawthorn trees close to the road. Further on, under the large farm building, the walk goes through woodland of deciduous oaks.

The large farm building is called **Cortijo de los Prados**, the farmhouse of the meadows, and the area around it is Huerto Alegre, the happy kitchen gardens. The establishment is a school for farm husbandry.

This area is very popular at the weekends with families coming to picnic and people walking and pony trekking.

◄ The dirt-track road runs out to the main road and the restaurant, from where it is a short hike back up to the start of the walk.

WALKS FROM THE NORTH

The walk under the high sandstone cliffs of the Alhama gorge (Walk 21)

To the north of the mountains of Nerja the land is elevated, being in excess of 900m. From Ventas de Zafarraya over to Alhama de Granada it is a virtual flat plateau of fertile land that receives more rainfall than the coast. During the heat of the summer the temperature here is more bearable.

Five walks are included here, two of them virtually flat and with two long treks into the heart of the mountains. The first walk described, divided into two sections, at Ventas de Zafarraya, makes for two spectacular short hikes.

WALK 19
Ventas de Zafarraya

Start/Finish	parking area just after the pass, Ventas de Zafarraya
Distance	western loop: 5km; eastern loop: 5km
Difficulty	western loop: 4; eastern loop: 3
Time	western loop: 1½ hrs; eastern loop: 2hrs
Height gain	western loop: 260m; eastern loop: 325m
Getting there	Both walks begin at a parking area immediately on the left after going through the pass and before entering the village (if you are coming from the coast).
Options	Combining both walks makes the visit to Zafarraya more meaningful, and lunch can be taken between the two.
Note	Within a classical col of these proportions the wind speeds can be high and the temperature cold. Clouds very often tend to engulf these mountains.

This route describes a walk of two halves – the first on the western side of the pass and the second on the eastern side – that can easily be combined with lunch at the pass to make a full day. The scenery is amazing up here, including the huge cave at the summit of the western walk, and you may see falcons on the eastern loop.

Ventas de Zafarraya is at the pass (*boquete* or *puerto*) through the Sierra Tejeda that affords

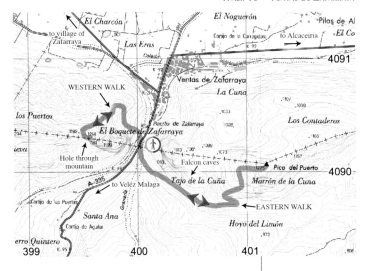

passage into the great plains of the northern Axarquía. The pass is at an elevation of 900m. During the time of the Phoenicians the River Vélez

The mountain pass at Ventas de Zafarraya

was navigable up to Vélez-Málaga. This allowed invaders to come in from the sea and the route up through the Zafarraya pass provided good access to Granada.

In the early part of the last century there was a narrow gauge steam railway that connected the villages of La Viñuela, Periana and Zafarraya to Vélez-Málaga and Torre del Mar. The railway was to eventually connect Granada to the sea, but in 1928 the plans were abandoned.

Western loop

The western walk is a waymarked route into the Sierra Alhama. The path leads up the mountain beside the sendero information sign (elevation: 930m). This is a tough little climb. It will take 30mins to arrive at the first viewing point, Mirador de los Pradillos, and a further 20mins or so before it reaches the summit.

The limestone forms **tall chimneys** on this exposed path. These limestones are of Jurassic origin, much younger than the limestones of Maroma through to Navachica.

Near the summit you have to clamber blindly over bare rock until what looks like an enormous cave comes into view. Descending for a closer look, it will become clear that it is not in fact a cave but a massive hole through the mountain.

From the **summit**, at 1190m, there is a panoramic view, southwards to the sea, westwards to the Viñuela reservoir and beyond to the mountains of Malaga, eastwards to the hulk of La Maroma, and northwards to the fertile plains of Alhama de Granada.

Return the same way. On the descent the stony path can be slippery. On the side of the path are very prickly, yet delicate, Andalucían thistles.

Eastern loop

On the opposite side of the road and below the pass is the start of the eastern walk. ▶ The walk goes under the **Tajo de la Cuña**, the cliff face of the wedge, to circle and climb up to Pico de Puerto (1225m), the top of the pass.

Start on a wide dirt track that presently, after a boulder, becomes a narrow path where the vegetation gradually makes walking more difficult. **Note** This is not a walk for shorts.

Note that this is over private land but there are no signs forbidding access.

> The **views** over the countryside are equally as stunning on this side of the pass as they are on the opposite side, and there are many caves and holes through the mountain. The second cliff face that is passed has caves in which peregrine falcons nest. The birds may be seen soaring overhead or calling warnings of intruders.

Peregrine falcon

After two zig-zags the made path comes to an end. From there a narrower path proceeds over the vegetation, a relatively short distance, to a col between two peaks that is referred to as La Cuna, the cradle. Now the bare limestone can be scaled to the summit of **Pico del Puerto**, where the view can be savoured. Return the same way.

Pico del Puerto

WALK 20

Malascamas

Start/Finish	road junction ½ km from Cortijo de los Nacimientos at 1026:414522:4088330
Distance	18km to the col; 19km to the summit
Difficulty	6 to the col; 8 to the summit
Time	5½ hrs to the col; 6½ hrs to the summit
Height gain	621m to the col; 762m to the summit
Getting there	The objective is to arrive at Cortijo de los Nacimientos, the farmhouse of the (water) sources (rivers and ravines) at 950:414450:4088175. Drive from Alcaicería towards Alhama de Granada; just before the town of Alhama take the road to the right for Jatar and Arenas del Rey; pass by a reservoir; 5½ km past the reservoir take the paved road to the right; this road leads to a large farming area and a quarry (in 2013 the farm was signposted La Patilla); after the quarry the road turns to a dirt-track; at the first fork take the left-hand option, following the main dirt-track; presently the road arrives at a junction at 1026:414522:4088330, where the roads ahead are narrower. Park at this junction.
Note	At 19km this is the longest route in this guide and it will take all day. The hostelries at Alcaicería and at the Alhama reservoir are good and convenient places to spend the night. Attention to the route is important and a GPS is essential to find the starting point.

This is a classic walk, with all the ingredients for a good day's hike – relatively straightforward, but varied and interesting. You reach Malascamas via a grassy col just under the summit. From this col all the views are available but if you want to bag the summit there is a difficult passage over loose scree and a scramble to the top.

At 1792m Malascamas, 'the bad beds' in Spanish, is the highest of the intermediate group of mountains between La Maroma and Cerro de la Chapa. It cannot be seen from Nerja. Like La Maroma it is remote, being over 9km from a place where a car can travel to and considerably further away from a paved road. Contrary to what any map may imply there is no path to the summit from the northwest, so that a circular walk is not a possibility. Malascamas can also be approached from the south from La Fabrica de la Luz.

Road route to the Barranco

Take the road to the left from the parking area and proceed to some gates where there are signs indicating private land. Walk around the gates and proceed to another set, with more signs about private land. However, to the left of these second gates is the old road into the Barranco. It continues up to a third set of gates and below this the river and the old camino through Barranco de Malinfierno can be seen. The route is marked clearly on the maps and a GPS will help to confirm this.

Riverside route to the Barranco

The road straight ahead of the parking area drops down to the river under Cortijo de los Nacimientos – the farmhouse of the (water) sources (rivers and ravines). This river is the Rio Alhama and the route is to follow this river to its source. From here there is initially no trail, but eventually walking alongside the river is relatively straightforward. The river is coming out of the Barranco de Malinfierno. Barranco de Malinfierno means the 'ravine of the bad hell', but the ravine is actually a very pleasant route to walk. It is a 4km trek following the river. In the mornings the barranco is shaded from the sun. Peaks will come into view but none of them are Malascamas – you don't get your first glimpse until after you've emerged from the ravine.

> This was a proper path that a cart could negotiate, but floods have destroyed it in a number of places. The severest flood in the past few decades occurred in September 2007 when over 200mm of rain fell within 24 hours. **Note** This is an ancient route and

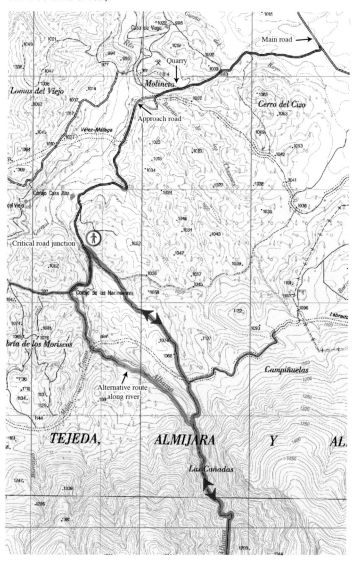

Main road

Quarry

Molineta

Cerro del Cizo

Lomas del Viejo

Vélez-Málaga

Approach road

Cortijo Casa Alta

del Viejo

Critical road junction

Cortijo de los Nacimientos

bría de los Moriscos

Alternative route along river

Campiñuelas

TEJEDA, ALMIJARA Y AL

Las Cañadas

although it is no longer possible to travel over it, it is a public right-of-way. The lands on either side of the road are private but the owners are more interested in preserving their hunting rights than in interfering with walkers.

Entrance to the Barranco de Malinfierno

The path diverts away from the river in places, but eventually returns. Two-thirds of the way into the Barranco the brown limestone is prone to erosion and the river has caused the rock to collapse. Eventually the path arrives at a virtual oasis in the wilderness.

This is **Haza del Aguadero**, an extensive farm, now sadly dilapidated. Here is the source of the Río Alhama, the same river that cuts through the gorge of Alhama, travels north collecting tributaries and expands to a mighty river before discharging into the great lake at Iznájar. From the farm the mountains appear to form a long ridge line stretching away to the west. The peak at the far end of this ridge is Malascamas.

The summit of Malascamas with La Maroma ahead

At **Haza del Aguadero** the direction changes to due west, following a dirt-track path that zig-zags into the mountains. This valley is **Hoya de Gutiérrez**. The rise is gradual. After 2km ignore the path to the right and continue to a grassy col at 1651m.

From the col **La Maroma** can be seen in all its splendour. Above the col to the right of Maroma is the trigonometric station that is the summit of Malascamas (1792m).

There is no easy path to the summit. Off the dirt track and swinging away to the right of the col there is the semblance of a goat track. This leads to the summit from the rear. The alternative is to opt for a full-frontal climb. The best option is to go up the steep way and come down on the goat track.

The top of the ridge is a series of jagged **limestone outcrops**. Perhaps this is where the name 'bad beds' comes from. At the summit a distinct path can be seen proceeding from the grassy col all the way over and up Maroma.

On the descent the journey can be shortened by coming off track to bypass the many hairpins.

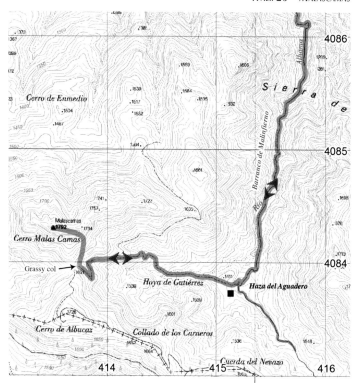

Haza del Aguadero is a pleasant place to rest. This farm was fully working until the great 2007 flood. With the track into it severed it sounded the death knell for the place. Now the only inhabitant is a shepherd who manages a herd of goats. The crocuses that are common in northern Europe in the spring bloom here in the autumn.

At the bottom of Barranco de Malinfierno, choose either the riverside or the road route to return to your car.

WALK 21

The Gorge of Alhama de Granada

Start/Finish	tourist office beside the town hall, Alhama de Granada
Distance	6km
Difficulty	1
Time	2½ hrs
Height gain	110m
Options	Return back up through the town instead of along the road above the gorge.

'One of the unsung gems of the Granada Province' is how the Rough Guide to Andalucía refers to Alhama de Granada. The town is at an elevation of 1000m and has had a dwindling population for a number of decades. It is perched over a gorge and the route begins by walking through this gorge and returning on the opposite cliff top.

This route is waymarked as the 'Sendero de Termalismo'.

The **tourist office** provides free maps of the town and brochures of the attractions in the area. Housed in a nearby building is a collection of old photographs showing the lives of local people over the years.

Go to the left of the tourist office and around to the rear to look down into the gorge, and take the second set of steps. At the bottom of the steps are the ruins of one of the five flour mills of Alhama, but going further down to explore them is not very interesting. So, turn to the right and proceed along under the daunting cliff.

These horizontally bedded **Miocene sandstones** are only 15 million years old, so they post-date the mountain-building era of Southern Andalucía. Old

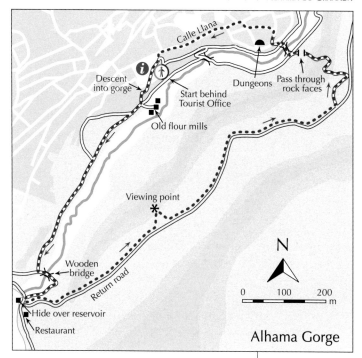

Alhama Gorge

farm buildings, and a 16th-century church, have been cut into the soft rock.

En route watch out for the **pilas de lavar**, stones shaped to assist women washing clothes. Further along a noticeboard tells the legend of 'The Leap of the Horse'.

Eventually the path reaches and crosses a wooden bridge and goes out to the main road. Turn left and walk along the road to a shaded area, where there is a bird-watcher's hide that overlooks the reservoir. ▶

Across the main road from the hide take the paved road that goes left (there is a signpost for the Camino de Termalismo). This is a little-used road that climbs gently

At this point an alternative would be to go back along the main road and walk into town on a path above the gorge.

135

Immediately beyond this pass the walk turns to the right

to the far side of the gorge. Halfway along the road there is a mirador, a viewing point that looks down into the gorge and over to the town.

Continue along the road and presently follow a sign that points down into the gorge again. After the path goes through a pass in the rocks take the first path on the right (see photo). This climbs up steep steps to emerge at the **dungeons**.

> The '**dungeons**' are large vaulted structures that were originally created by the Moors for grain storage, but they were also used for other purposes, such as the incarceration of prisoners during the Civil War.

Beyond the dungeons there is a narrow lane that leads up to one of Alhama's longest streets. Calle Llana connects a square at the eastern end of town to Plaza Santiago at the western end. Turn left to return to the tourist office.

WALK 22
La Resinera

Start/Finish	La Resinera interpretive centre, near Fornes
Distance	11km
Difficulty	1
Time	3hrs
Height gain	330m
Getting there	From Arenas del Rey head in the direction of the village of Fornes, but short of the village follow the sign for La Resinera.
Options	Exploring the village of Fornes.

This is a gentle circular half-day route through peaceful countryside with a high chance of seeing some red deer. It is waymarked and officially suitable for wheelchair users but the length, rough surfaces and the gradients belie such a classification.

La Resinera is one of two interpretive centres in the Nature Park – the other is in Sedella. In the centre, which is housed in a former church building, there are visual displays about the local plants and wildlife and interactive displays about the local history and way of life. A visit is highly recommended.

Take the dirt track road to the right of the centre, which drops down to the river. This is a popular picnic spot where people come to bathe in the River Cacín. Cross the bridge and proceed out into the country. Presently the road comes to another river, never more than a trickle, that must be crossed.

> The walk is under cliffs of soft **sandstone**. These sandstones are young in geological terms, being of Quaternary age.

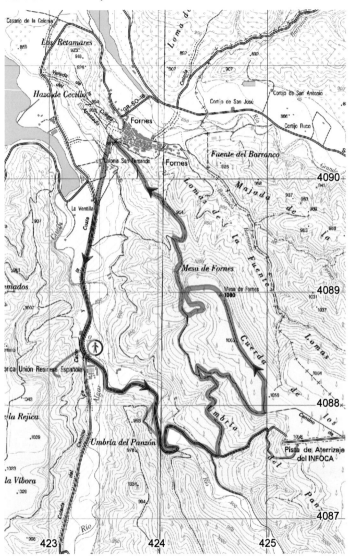

THE RESIN INDUSTRY

The visitor centre

When a pine tree is cut it oozes resin, the sticky liquid assisting in healing the wound. In the late 19th and 20th centuries this resin was a commercial product with many uses. Pine trees were cut in regular patterns and cups affixed to save the oozing resin. Sierra Tejeda takes its name from the word Tejo, meaning yew, and, before the resin industry began to flourish, all of the yews were cut down to make way for pines. The yews were also considered poisonous to livestock. At the height of resin production many thousands of people were employed in the industry.

Cross open flat ground to arrive at **Mesa de Fornes**, the table of Fornes. Here, halfway through the walk, there is a trig point and, west of it, an old lookout structure.

The walk has arrived at the **halfway point**, deep in the country, with only the sounds of the country audible. In the summer this area becomes scorched and all of the vegetation turns brown and withered, only to rise dramatically again at the first rains.

This is the bend in the route above Fornes. The walk arrives on the left and leaves to the right

The path narrows and is defined by white painted rocks on either side. Crossing the plateau there are fine views over to the reservoir, Embalse de los Bermejales, and to the village of **Fornes**. The path drops down and arrives at the upper section of the village. There is a sharp turn here and you take the road to the left.

The waymarks lead past housing onto a narrow path that runs alongside an irrigation channel. Eventually it emerges onto the dirt-track road to La Resinera, where you need to turn left.

WALK 23

Jayena to Haza de la Encina

Start/Finish	Bacal recreation area, Jayena
Distance	9km
Difficulty	3
Time	3hrs
Height gain	360m
Getting there	To get to Jayena from the coast is probably quicker via Almuñécar and Otívar, rather than Ventas de Zafarraya. Once there, follow the signs for the recreation area of Bacal. You have to ford the river as you approach the campsite, but the water will be shallow.
Options	There is another walk in Jayena alongside the river.
Note	This route is supposed to be waymarked but it is not consistently so. There are a few waymarks at the beginning and at the end, but none in the middle, so take care to follow the paths.

Jayena is a remote village in the northeast corner of the area covered by this guide. The village is surrounded by olive groves and the major industry here is the harvesting of olives. Being at an elevation of 900m, the climate is a little more temperate than down on the coast.

There is one linear road through the campsite and the walk sets out on this, initially following the River Bacal in a southeasterly direction and then turning up to go south through a ravine, Rambla de la Cuerda de los Morros, the route of the rope of the Moors. It emerges to a viewpoint over the eastern Almijaras.

The **Bacal recreation area** is quite an extensive site beside the river, has all the basic camping facilities and is very quiet.

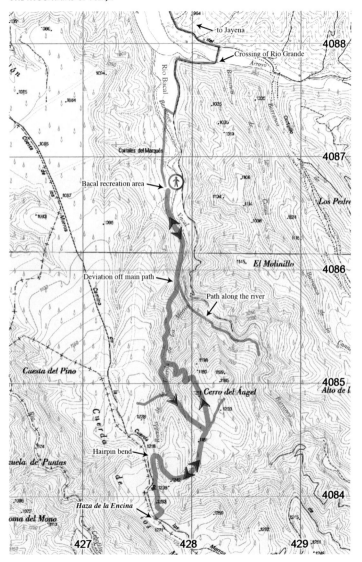

to Jayena

Crossing of Río Grande

4088

Río Bacal

4087

Corrales del Marqués

Bacal recreation area

Los Pedre

El Molinillo

4086

Deviation off main path

Path along the river

Cuesta del Pino

4085

Cerro del Ángel

Alto de l

Hairpin bend

4084

Haza de la Encina

oma del Mono

427   428   429

Start from the signpost at the campsite. The sign says that it is 4½ km to the vantage point and the same to return. This is about right.

Within and beyond the campsite, in spring **tiny daffodils** may be blooming on the side of the path. They are only a few inches in height.

A little over a kilometre from the campsite there is a sign indicating the way to Haza de la Encina. ▶

The path climbs up to circle south into the ravine and comes to a path junction at 1060:427727:4085165. Both paths lead to the same destination. The official path from this point is the lower one to the left that travels along the eastern side of the ravine (without waymarks) and is the more strenuous option.

Take the path to the right, which is less well trodden and travels along the western side of the ravine. Follow it as it enters and then meanders through the pine forest. It drops to the bottom of the ravine and proceeds along it for some distance. At 1100:427865:4084800 it emerges onto a dirt track where you turn left. A little further reach another dirt track at a T-junction (1130:428110:4084600) and turn right. ▶

Hairpin bend at the firebreak. Your destination is on the right

Encina is the Spanish for Holm Oak and lots of them will be passed en route.

This is deer country. There are no cabras montés about, but there are plenty of red deer.

143

The sendero signpost

Soon the path reaches an area where there is an extensive firebreak and meets yet another dirt track where a waymark points left (at a hairpin bend, see photo). The vista ahead is of the back of the Almijaras. Just a little walk along this road reaches another waymark (right) and a viewpoint.

At the **viewpoint** (1260:427615:4083760) there is a plaque pinpointing the features of the landscape. Cerro de Cabaneros (1717m) is impressive, but it is only the extension of Navachica (1832m) behind it. The solitary cone of Lucero is there and to its right the hulk of Cerro de la Chapa.

To return, walk back to the hairpin bend and the T-junction but this time carry on straight ahead to a cairn at 1145:428080:4084690, which invites the walker to take the path on the left, which will lead back to the start. The return journey has many zig-zags and the advantage to stay high at that initial path junction becomes clearer.

CISNE

WALK 24
Cisne from Acebuchal

Start/Finish	Acebuchal
Distance	19km
Difficulty	10
Time	8hrs
Height gain	983m
Getting there	Passing through Frigiliana on the road towards Cómpeta, there is a sign at 3.5km indicating Acebuchal to the right. After a further 2.5km the road reaches the village. Park just short of the village at a ravine on the right.
Options	Instead of returning to Acebuchal via the ravine you could return along the road. This option is 3km longer but it includes a fine view down over the village. With a 4WD vehicle you could drive all the way to the base of the mountain and back by road. To do this, turn off on a dirt track on the right a kilometre before the village.

There are other mountains and then there is Cisne. This is the most difficult of the mountains of Nerja. Often referred to as the K2 of Andalucía, it is a mere 1483m in height, but to climb it requires particular mountaineering skills. The difficulty rating of 10 is well merited – to summit Cisne involves a long walk in and out, scrambling over precipitous rock, manoeuvring through loose, steep scree and climbing the last 700m in under 3km.

Resistance to the Franco regime continued in some parts of Andalucía for many years after the civil war ended. The Maqui found sanctuary in the mountain villages and settlements. Indeed it was as late as 1948 that the Guardia Civilia cleared **Acebuchal** and destroyed the village. The name of the village comes from acebuche, the wild olive tree. With the aid of grants from the government of Andalucía, the village has now been almost fully restored.

It is important to remember this junction on the way back or you may overshoot and add 1½ km to your journey.

Follow the ravine to its end, a little over 2km from the start. Here (620:418370:4076100) you emerge onto one of two dirt tracks. Join the one that goes north. ◀

Half a kilometre later come to the ruin of **Venta Cebollero**. Take the track to the right immediately beyond this building. Ignoring the next track to the right, continue up a wide ravine to re-join the main dirt track just short of Collado Blanquilla (which is at 813:419357:4077520). The first view of Cisne emerges above this pass but unfortunately the walk loses elevation after this before starting the climb proper.

After a kilometre the dirt track road reaches a road junction. Take the road to the right signposted Vereda del Puerto de los Umbrales. Walking down the dirt track, a path can be seen crossing the base of Cisne, which goes to the col known as **Puerto de los Umbrales**. Do not take this; keep following the dirt track.

Presently the road comes to a reservoir over a river. This river is the **Rio Higueron** that passes to the side of Frigiliana to join the Rio Chillar just outside of Nerja.

Venta Cebollero

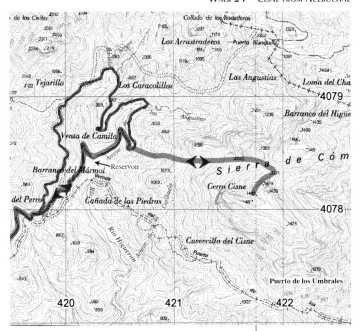

Following the main dirt track that passes the reservoir, cross the river a second time and walk up a concrete road.

The start of the track up Cisne is well marked (800:420630:4078545). Indeed, the route to the summit is very well marked via small cairns and coloured spots. The track is narrow and steep. At 1000m you can take a breather at a col, and then another at 1200m.

> On the ascent you may be wondering whether the daunting **cliffs** ahead have to be scaled, but you will eventually be able to see that the route goes to the left to circle around them.

The path arrives at a col on the north side of the summit. This col is Collado de Dos Hermanos (the col of the

149

two brothers). The path now traverses under the cliff on the eastern side of the summit to reach a gully that leans up to the summit. Negotiating the bare rock into the gully is precipitous and must be carried out with care, for this is the most dangerous part of the climb. **Roping up for safety is recommended.**

Once inside the gully, the climb is steep but relatively safe. ◄

Emerge onto the flat area at the top of the gully with a sign of relief!

There is a cave on the right that would be a welcome shelter should the weather turn for the worse.

> There appears to be a choice of three **summits**, set out in a triangle. The one straight ahead and slightly to the left is the highest point (1483m) and it is an easy scramble over rock to reach it. From the summit there is a good view down over Frigiliana to Nerja and the coast. A look back at Lucero clearly shows the lookout structure on its summit.

The mountaineer's rule that descending should be handled with more care than the ascent is very appropriate on Cisne. The scree will slide under your boots; particular care is required making the transition from the gulley to the path; and below this watching carefully for the little cairns is of paramount importance. There is one particular gully on the descent that it is essential to leave at the right point – if you follow it all the way down you will have to climb back because there is no exit below (apart from a 4m vertical drop).

Perspiration can be washed off in the river at the base before starting the long trudge back to Acebuchal. After passing Venta Cebollero watch out for the entry into the ravine. If you miss it, returning by road provides a fine aerial view of Acebuchal.

APPENDIX A
Route summary table

No	Name	Nearest town	Distance (km)	Time (hrs)	Difficulty	Page
Nerja and around						
Walk 1	Frigiliana to the Cave of Nerja	Frigiliana	15	5½	3	30
Walk 2	El Fuerte	Frigiliana	9	3½	4	38
Walk 3	La Cruz del Pinto	Nerja	8	4½	2	44
Walk 4	The Gorges of the Rio Chillar	Nerja	15	4	3	48
Walk 5	The El Cielo Circuit	Nerja	14	7	8	52
Walk 6	The tour of Almendrón	Nerja	13	5	8½	57
The Cómpeta Area						
Walk 7	La Fabrica de la Luz	Cómpeta	11½	4	2	64
Walk 8	Lucero	Cómpeta	12	4½	5	69
Walk 9	Cerro de la Chapa	Cómpeta	9½	4½	4	73
Walk 10	The oak forest of Salares	Salares	7	3½	3	77
Walk 11	Cómpeta to Los Pradillos	Cómpeta	15	5	3	81
La Maroma						
Walk 12	La Maroma from Canillas de Aceituno	Canillas de Aceituno	19	7½	7	91
Walk 13	La Maroma from Alcaucín	Alcaucín	15	6½	8	96

No	Name	Nearest town	Distance (km)	Time (hrs)	Difficulty	Page
Walk 14	La Maroma from Sedella	Sedella	22	8½	8½	100
Walk 15	La Maroma from Alcaicería	Alcaicería	15	5	6	105
The Valley of the Rio Verde						
Walk 16	Navachica	Nerja	17	7½	7	110
Walk 17	The Petrified Waterfall	Otivar	10	3	3	115
Walk 18	Lopera	Otivar	8	3	1	119
Walks from the North						
Walk 19	Ventas de Zafarraya	Ventas de Zafarraya	10	3½	3½	124
Walk 20	Malascamas	Alhama de Granada	19	6½	8	128
Walk 21	The Gorge of Alhama de Granada	Alhama de Granada	6	2½	1	134
Walk 22	La Resinera	Fornes	11	3	1	137
Walk 23	Jayena to Haza de la Encina	Jayena	9	3	3	141
Cisne						
Walk 24	Cisne from Acebuchal	Cómpeta	19	8	10	146

APPENDIX B

List of peaks by altitude

The following is a list of the peaks in order of altitude in the area covered by this guide (roughly bounded by the roads A-7, A-356, A-402, GR-141, SO-31 and the SO-02). Where there are summits in close proximity to each other or summits that follow a ridge then only the highest point is included here. There are many peaks that are unnamed and these have not been included.

1	La Maroma	2069m		26	El Cielo	1508m
2	Navachica	1831m		27	Enmedio	1504m
3	Selledero	1829m		28	El Fuerte 1	1503m
4	Tojo Fuerte	1826m		29	Lopera	1485m
5	La Chapa	1818m		30	Cisne	1483m
6	Malascamas	1792m		31	El Sol (near Almendrón)	1478m
7	La Majada del Arce	1789m		32	Alto Ubares	1399m
8	Lucero	1774m		33	Buitrera	1378m
9	Albucaz	1726m		34	Chupa	1352m
10	Cabañeros	1716m		35	Verde 1	1329m
11	La Venta Panaderos	1687m		36	Alto la Teja	1325m
12	Piedra Sillada	1678m		37	Alto del Aguila	1325m
13	Mota	1649m		38	Pico de Puerto	1228m
14	Santiago	1645m		39	Martos	1222m
15	La Cadena	1645m		40	Rodoceros	1207m
16	Los Llanos	1644m		41	Panizo	1201m
17	Tajadillas Oscuras	1642m		42	Capriote	1145m
18	Tacica del Plata	1639m		43	Naranjo	1140m
19	Alto de los Buitres	1615m		44	Escala	1108m
20	Los Majanos	1605m		45	Umbria de los Moriscos	1181m
21	Los Corrales	1596m		46	Gallego	1074m
22	Los Machos	1589m		47	Cizo	1070m
23	Cenacho	1527m		48	El Fuerte 2	1007m
24	Peñon Rodado	1522m		49	Monderos	930m
25	Loma la Chaparral	1516m		50	Verde 2	918m

APPENDIX C

Useful Spanish words for map reading

abandonada	disused, abandoned	nacimiento	birth, source (of a river)
altura	altitude		
arroyo	stream	peñón	crag, rocky outcrop
barranco	ravine	pozo	Water well
cabra	goat	pradillos	small meadows
calera	limestone quarry/kiln	prados	meadows
camino	path, track	puerta	gate
campo	field, country	puerto	a port, but in this case a mountain pass
cantera	quarry		
cascada	waterfall	rambla	dry river bed, but also boulevard
cazador	hunter		
cerro	mountain, hill	raspón	groove or scrape (suggesting a track cut into the landscape)
chapa	linen, but also badge and cap		
collado	pass	tajo	face, cliff (rock face of a mountain)
cortijo	country farm house		
cruz	cross	vereda	path
cuerda	string, rope		
cuesta	hill, shoulder		
cueva	cave		
cuna	cradle, col		
cuña	wedge		
embalse	reservoir		
encina	evergreen oak – holm oak		
fuente	well, spring, fountain		
haza	plot of arable land		
goya	river basin, valley		
llano	plain, area of flat ground		
loma	hill, hillock		
maroma	rope		
mirador	vantage point, lookout		
mojón	marker, boundary stone		

APPENDIX D
Further reading

General information
Sierras de Tejeda, Almijara y Alhama Manuel Clavero Salvador, Cornicabra, 2011. The official guide to the Axarquía, in Spanish. Excellent publication. Very well illustrated. Maps included.

La Axarquía – Land to the East of Málaga Hilary Gavilan, Discovery Walking Guides, 2008. This book, in English, describes the history and culture of the Axarquía.

Spanish wildflowers
Flores Silvestres de Andalucía Gabriel Garcí Guardia, Editorial Rueda, 1988. A guide, in Spanish, to wildflowers, but mainly at low level. Well illustrated, but no cross-references to northern European flowers.

Common Wildflowers of Spain Austen F Colwell, Santana, 2008. Few specific mountain flowers of Andalucía are included. Some of the flowers are cross-referenced in Spanish.

The descent from Cisne is over scree, through gullies and narrow paths (Walk 24)

APPENDIX E

Maps of the region

Topografica 1:50,000

These are the Spanish equivalent of Ordnance Survey maps, of which four are required for this area: 1040, 1041, 1054 and 1055. Not freely available but can be purchased in Malaga from Mapas y Compania, on Calle Compania, and also online. Poor quality paper so limited life.

Topografica 1:25,000

Larger scale. The maps are gridded in metric, but also have the imperial outline in the margins. There are four maps to every one of the four 1:50,000 scale sheets, so 16 maps to cover the entire area. Poor quality paper so limited life.

Discovery Tour and Trail 1:40,000

2010 version issued with Charles Davis' walks marked onto it. Imperial grid only. Very clear and easy to follow, but contains a number of minor errors.

Mapa Topografica 1:75,000

Miguel Angel Torres Delgado 2002. Gridded in metric, but the detail is poor; paths and dirt tracks are difficult to follow.

Geological maps

The Instituto Geologico Y Minero de España publish 1:200,000 maps of the Iberian Peninsula and the mountains of Nerja are within the scope of Map 83.

Acebuchal (Walk 24)

LISTING OF CICERONE GUIDES

SCOTLAND
Backpacker's Britain:
   Northern Scotland
Ben Nevis and Glen Coe
Cycling in the Hebrides
Great Mountain Days in Scotland
Mountain Biking in Southern and
   Central Scotland
Mountain Biking in West and
   North West Scotland
Not the West Highland Way
   Scotland
Scotland's Best Small Mountains
Scotland's Far West
Scotland's Mountain Ridges
Scrambles in Lochaber
The Ayrshire and Arran
   Coastal Paths
The Border Country
The Cape Wrath Trail
The Great Glen Way
The Great Glen Way Map Booklet
The Hebridean Way
The Hebrides
The Isle of Mull
The Isle of Skye
The Skye Trail
The Southern Upland Way
The Speyside Way
The Speyside Way Map Booklet
The West Highland Way
Walking Highland Perthshire
Walking in Scotland's Far North
Walking in the Angus Glens
Walking in the Cairngorms
Walking in the Ochils, Campsie
   Fells and Lomond Hills
Walking in the Pentland Hills
Walking in the Southern Uplands
Walking in Torridon
Walking Loch Lomond and
   the Trossachs
Walking on Arran
Walking on Harris and Lewis
Walking on Jura, Islay
   and Colonsay
Walking on Rum and the
   Small Isles
Walking on the Orkney and
   Shetland Isles
Walking on Uist and Barra
Walking the Corbetts
   Vol 1 South of the Great Glen
Walking the Corbetts
   Vol 2 North of the Great Glen
Walking the Galloway Hills
Walking the Munros
   Vol 1 – Southern, Central and
   Western Highlands

Walking the Munros
   Vol 2 – Northern Highlands
   and the Cairngorms
West Highland Way Map Booklet
Winter Climbs Ben Nevis and
   Glen Coe
Winter Climbs in the Cairngorms

NORTHERN ENGLAND TRAILS
Hadrian's Wall Path
Hadrian's Wall Path Map Booklet
Pennine Way Map Booklet
The Coast to Coast Map Booklet
The Coast to Coast Walk
The Dales Way
The Pennine Way

LAKE DISTRICT
Cycling in the Lake District
Great Mountain Days in the
   Lake District
Lake District Winter Climbs
Lake District:
   High Level and Fell Walks
Lake District:
   Low Level and Lake Walks
Lakeland Fellranger series
Mountain Biking in the
   Lake District
Scrambles in the Lake District
   – North
Scrambles in the Lake District
   – South
Short Walks in Lakeland
   Books 1, 2 and 3
The Cumbria Coastal Way
The Cumbria Way
Tour of the Lake District
Trail and Fell Running in the
   Lake District

NORTH WEST ENGLAND AND
THE ISLE OF MAN
Cycling the Pennine Bridleway
Isle of Man Coastal Path
The Lancashire Cycleway
The Lune Valley and Howgills –
   A Walking Guide
The Ribble Way
Walking in Cumbria's Eden Valley
Walking in Lancashire
Walking in the Forest of
   Bowland and Pendle
Walking on the Isle of Man
Walking on the West
   Pennine Moors
Walks in Lancashire
   Witch Country
Walks in Ribble Country

Walks in Silverdale and Arnside
Walks in the Forest of Bowland

NORTH EAST ENGLAND,
YORKSHIRE DALES AND
PENNINES
Cycling in the Yorkshire Dales
Great Mountain Days in
   the Pennines
Historic Walks in North Yorkshire
Mountain Biking in the
   Yorkshire Dales
South Pennine Walks
St Oswald's Way and
   St Cuthbert's Way
The Cleveland Way and the
   Yorkshire Wolds Way
The Cleveland Way Map Booklet
The North York Moors
The Reivers Way
The Teesdale Way
Walking in County Durham
Walking in Northumberland
Walking in the North Pennines
Walking in the Yorkshire Dales:
   North and East
Walking in the Yorkshire Dales:
   South and West
Walks in Dales Country
Walks in the Yorkshire Dales

WALES AND WELSH BORDERS
Glyndwr's Way
Great Mountain Days
   in Snowdonia
Hillwalking in Shropshire
Hillwalking in Wales – Vol 1
Hillwalking in Wales – Vol 2
Mountain Walking in Snowdonia
Offa's Dyke Path
Offa's Dyke Map Booklet
Pembrokeshire Coast Path
   Map Booklet
Ridges of Snowdonia
Scrambles in Snowdonia
The Ascent of Snowdon
The Ceredigion and Snowdonia
   Coast Paths
The Pembrokeshire Coast Path
The Severn Way
The Snowdonia Way
The Wales Coast Path
The Wye Valley Walk
Walking in Carmarthenshire
Walking in Pembrokeshire
Walking in the Forest of Dean
Walking in the South
   Wales Valleys
Walking in the Wye Valley

For full information on all our
guides, books and eBooks,
visit our website:
www.cicerone.co.uk

Walking – Trekking – Mountaineering – Climbing - Cycling

Over 40 years, Cicerone have built up an outstanding collection of over 300 guides, inspiring all sorts of amazing adventures.

Every guide comes from extensive exploration and research by our expert authors, all with a passion for their subjects. They are frequently praised, endorsed and used by clubs, instructors and outdoor organisations.

All our titles can now be bought as **e-books**, **ePubs** and **Kindle** files and we also have an online magazine – **Cicerone Extra** – with features to help cyclists, climbers, walkers and trekkers choose their next adventure, at home or abroad.

Our website shows any **new information** we've had in since a book was published. Please do let us know if you find anything has changed, so that we can publish the latest details. On our **website** you'll also find great ideas and lots of detailed information about what's inside every guide and you can buy **individual routes** from many of them online.

It's easy to keep in touch with what's going on at Cicerone by getting our monthly **free e-newsletter**, which is full of offers, competitions, up-to-date information and topical articles. You can subscribe on our home page and also follow us on **Facebook** and **Twitter** or dip into our **blog**.

Cicerone – the very best guides for exploring the world.

CICERONE

2 Police Square Milnthorpe Cumbria LA7 7PY
Tel: 015395 62069 info@cicerone.co.uk
www.cicerone.co.uk and **www.cicerone-extra.com**